UNPACKING COMPLEXITY
IN INFORMATIONAL TEXTS

Also from Sunday Cummins

*Close Reading of Informational Texts:
Assessment-Driven Instruction in Grades 3–8*

For more information, visit the author's website:
www.Sunday-Cummins.com

Unpacking Complexity in Informational Texts

PRINCIPLES AND PRACTICES FOR GRADES 2–8

Sunday Cummins

Foreword by Elfrieda H. Hiebert

THE GUILFORD PRESS
New York   London

© 2015 The Guilford Press
A Division of Guilford Publications, Inc.
72 Spring Street, New York, NY 10012
www.guilford.com

Printed in the United States of America

This book is printed on acid-free paper.

Last digit is print number: 9   8   7   6   5   4   3   2   1

Library of Congress Cataloging-in-Publication Data is available from the publisher.

ISBN 978-1-4625-1859-3 (cloth)
ISBN 978-1-4625-1850-0 (paper)

About the Author

Sunday Cummins, PhD, is an independent literacy consultant who lives in Chico, California, and consults nationally. Formerly, she was Assistant Professor of Education in the Reading and Language Department at National Louis University and a facilitator for the New Schools Project at the Erikson Institute in Chicago. Before becoming a professor, Dr. Cummins worked in the public schools for 10 years as a middle school and third-grade teacher and as a literacy coach. She is the author of *Close Reading of Informational Texts: Assessment-Driven Instruction in Grades 3–8*, as well as articles in *The Reading Teacher* and *Educational Leadership*, and shares her work on teaching with informational texts by presenting at state, national, and international conferences. Her website is *www.Sunday-Cummins.com*.

Foreword

In the late 1990s, a 24/7 library opened on the Internet. More than 15 years later, this library is massive and increases in size daily. But it is not open to all. Lack of access to digital devices is one obstacle for many, but another obstacle as persistent and crucial is the technical proficiency required to use it. To make the best use of the explosive growth of information for the tasks of work, civic engagement, social interaction, and personal development, one needs to have a finely tuned set of strategies and skills.

Most of these strategies and skills are especially relevant to informational texts because these texts—whether traditional print books or unique new forms (e.g., graphic and oral presentations)—dominate in the digital–global age and play a central role in 21st-century classrooms. Simply providing students with informational texts is no longer sufficient, nor is engaging students in read-alouds of compelling texts or having them write the proverbial research report on animals (grade 2), plants (grade 3), states (grade 4), or countries (grade 5). Teachers now face the new demands of instructing students in acquiring knowledge and, even more important, acquiring it independently and at increasingly more complex levels.

The goal of the new-generation standards for English language arts (ELA), such as the Common Core State Standards, is to ensure that students have the capabilities and proficiencies for using texts to learn. But teachers need more than standards—they need to know how to select texts and create experiences that help their students acquire the skills and strategies to learn from complex informational texts. Teachers also need to understand how the structures and purposes of these texts contribute in essential ways to creating and communicating meaning.

In this timely book, Sunday Cummins addresses these critical issues. Several features of the book especially are important in understanding the nature of teaching for knowledge in today's classrooms. Its underlying theme is the need for teachers to understand what makes informational texts complex and unique. Authors of informational texts choose from a variety of text structures to organize content based on the purpose they have in mind. They assume a certain level of background knowledge on the part of their readers, they use a more formal tone than that frequently found in literary texts, and they use graphics, such as maps and charts, all of which make informational texts complex.

Another significant feature of informational texts is a more specialized vocabulary, which can be a persistent challenge for school-age readers encountering new content. Words, after all, are the means whereby ideas are communicated. Informational texts are written to convey unique ideas on specific topics, which means that readers can anticipate that an informational text on a particular topic will have a set of words that are likely to be unfamiliar. A text on gold can be expected to have words about characteristics (e.g., *malleable, ductile*) and processes (e.g., *dissolving, corrosion*), whereas a text on an archaeological find such as the terracotta warriors of ancient China has another unique vocabulary (e.g., *archaeologists, excavated, replica, figurines*). Authors of informational texts do not use synonyms for *archaeological* or *corrosion* but rather choose this unique vocabulary repeatedly to convey information accurately (Hiebert & Cervetti, 2012). When readers know that words critical to understanding the topic are repeated, they can anticipate that they might not understand a word on the first exposure but that they will have subsequent opportunities to learn more about a word's meaning as they move through the text.

Although Cummins does not develop this line of inquiry, the vocabulary of informational texts differs from that of literary texts in other ways. To communicate ideas about content, authors of informational texts often need to draw heavily on a group of words called general academic words (e.g., *compared, developed*). Many of these words are among the 2,500 complex word families that account for approximately 90% of the total words in both informational and literary texts (Hiebert, 2014). But frequency of a word should not be equated with ease of understanding. As the following two examples illustrate, a word may appear in both literary and informational writing, but the meaning can vary.

> James got into his own hammock and oh, how soft and comfortable it was compared with the hard bare boards that his aunts had always made him sleep upon at home. (Dahl, 1961, p. 13)

> This table compares how much a kid might weigh on the Moon, the Sun, and different planets. Which one has the strongest pull? (Beale, 2009, p. 17)

In the literature excerpt, *compare* conveys a noting of similarities and dissimilarities. In the informational text, the reader is asked to use the process of comparing to establish specific differences in measurement.

General academic words also are typically abstract and multisyllabic, features that can hinder students' ability to automatically recognize what the words mean. Moreover, the same form of a word can take on different functions (e.g., *progress* as a noun and verb). In informational texts, verbs can be transformed into nouns—a process called *nominalization*, a word that itself comes from a verb (*nominalize*). Other words have common meanings in everyday conversation but precise and technical meanings in content areas (e.g., *force*).

Often, general academic words are in the instructional background, while the content vocabulary of a topic is in the instructional foreground. To understand this unique vocabulary, however, requires a facility with general academic words since they are used to explain and describe ideas. The foregrounding of content vocabulary is to be expected in high school content-area classes, which is precisely why facility with general academic words needs to be developed by ELA teachers in the elementary and middle school grades.

Classrooms in which the aim is expanding students' capacity to comprehend increasingly more complex informational text should have many books, magazines, online resources, and so forth, for instructional enrichment. Students are acquiring funds of information as they read these materials. For example, after reading the book *The Emperor's Silent Army* (O'Connor, 2002), students will have learned about ancient cultures, in particular the nature of emperors in ancient China, and also about the critical role of artifacts in understanding ancient cultures.

Through reading informational texts, students gain new knowledge that in turn will serve them well as background knowledge for additional reading. Students will have a deeper understanding of *The Tale of the Mandarin Ducks* (Paterson, 1990) as a result of what they learned about Chinese emperors in *The Emperor's Silent Army* (O'Connor, 2002).

Increasing capacity for knowledge acquisition with informational texts, however, is not a substitute for in-depth content-area instruction. Through reading informational texts as part of ELA instruction, students can gain knowledge about a topic, but the emphasis in the ELA lesson is on the purpose of the text, the nature of vocabulary in the text, and the structure of sentences and paragraphs that the author uses to communicate aspects of the topic. However, with repeated exposure to the language and structures of complex text, students will be better able to absorb new content in social studies and science, whether it is the facets of different cultures or the elements of the periodic table, as they pursue a deeper knowledge.

As Sunday Cummins demonstrates, ELA teachers face challenges in determining how best to support students with complex informational texts. But the rewards are many. In particular, the compelling content of informational text—a terracotta army hidden for centuries, the training of rescue dogs, discoveries of new species in the deepest parts of oceans—all but guarantees student engagement. At the same time, students are acquiring a critical trove of information and a proficiency in reading increasingly complex texts in ways that underlie successful participation in the digital–global age. Here is the guidebook that teachers will want to use to design and implement lessons, tasks, and activities that unpack the complexity of informational texts and support students' capacity to access today's content-rich world successfully.

ELFRIEDA H. HIEBERT, PhD
TextProject and University of California, Santa Cruz

References

Beale, K. (2009). *Gravity is everywhere*. New York: Amplify.

Dahl, R. (1961). *James and the giant peach*. New York: Puffin Books.

Hiebert, E. H. (2014, July 19). *Development and application of a morphological family database in analyzing vocabulary patterns in texts*. Paper presented at the annual meeting of the Society for the Scientific Study of Reading, Santa Fe, NM.

Hiebert, E. H., & Cervetti, G. N. (2012). What differences in narrative and informational texts mean for the learning and instruction of vocabulary. In J. F. Baumann & E. J. Kame'enui (Eds.), *Vocabulary instruction: Research to practice* (2nd ed., pp. 322–344). New York: Guilford Press.

O'Connor, J. (2002). *The emperor's silent army: Terracotta warriors of ancient China*. New York: Viking Juvenile.

Paterson, K. (1990). *The tale of the Mandarin ducks*. New York: Puffin.

Contents

Introduction

THE ISSUE OF INFORMATIONAL TEXT COMPLEXITY

Take a moment to read the following excerpt from *Bones: Our Skeletal System* by renowned author Seymour Simon (2000). As you read, consider what you are learning about Simon's topic: the backbone.

> Your backbone, or spine, is a flexible column of bones that runs down the middle of your body. It is made up of a chain of thirty-three small bones called vertebrae, which are fastened one on top of another. Each vertebra is hard and hollow, like a bead or a spool of thread. The joint between each vertebra allows only a small amount of movement, but together the vertebrae form a flexible chain of bones that can twist like a string of beads. Your spine lets you bend down and touch your toes, and at the same time it keeps your body upright. (n.p.)[1]

In this one paragraph, Simon has developed a vivid picture of the backbone. He has included enough details about the physical features of the spine that we can understand why it allows us to bend down but not flop over. Simon writes skillfully with careful attention to detail, fully aware of his audience. Despite the clarity of the writing, there is still a lot of information and details for the reader to learn and retain. Many students would be overwhelmed by the task of "recalling" what they learned in this one paragraph, specifically because this is a complex text for them.

But what if, in order to learn Simon's content, these students understood how informational text authors such as Simon craft their texts? How the author has a *purpose*? How the purpose drives the author's *structure* of the text? How

---

[1] Excerpt from *Bones: Our Skeletal System*. Copyright © 2000 by Seymour Simon. Used by permission of HarperCollins Publishers. All rights reserved.

the author makes choices about using particular words and phrases that create a *cohesion* or logical flow of ideas? How this all contributes to the development of the author's *main ideas*?

Let me explain by returning to Simon's text for a closer analysis. The author has two purposes for the book from which this passage is excerpted. The first is *to describe* bones and groups of bones in our skeletal system and the second is *to explain* how these skeletal features help us. At the whole-text, or macro level, he uses an *enumerative text structure* in that he introduces a larger topic, the skeletal system, and then moves on to discuss subtopics such as the spine, the rib cage, and the bones of the arm. Each subtopic addressed contributes to a larger understanding of the larger topic, the skeletal system.

In the passage, Simon employs several *types of details* to describe the spine. He names the *subtopic* ("the backbone, or spine") and then gives us the *location* of this group of bones ("down the middle of your body"). He zooms in closer to the subtopic and identifies the *parts* of the backbone ("vertebrae") and *how many* there are ("thirty-three"). Then he addresses the *organization* of the vertebrae ("fastened one on top of another"), followed by a description of their *physical attributes* ("hard and hollow") and a *comparison* to an everyday object ("like a bead or a spool of thread"). All of these details are given in just the first three sentences of the passage.

In the last three sentences, the author returns to the larger subtopic, the spine, and makes a case for the spine's flexibility. The word *but* is an *adversative connective* that reveals the relationship between two ideas. Simon presents the idea that "each vertebra allows only a small amount of movement," and then, with the word *but*, he provides the contrasting idea that "together the vertebrae form a flexible chain of bones that can twist." He reinforces this fact with a comparison ("like a strong chain of beads"). The last sentence includes an *additive connective*, "at the same time," which reveals to the reader that the spine allows a person to "bend down and touch" her toes while also keeping her "body upright."

Finally, there is *cohesion* in this passage. The author's purpose, his structure of this passage (as well as the whole book), and the types of details and connective language he has chosen all contribute to the logical flow of ideas. If a reader can keep in mind the different aspects of this complex text that I have described, surely she would be more likely to understand and remember what she reads. What's more, the reader may grasp one of Simon's *main ideas*: that the spine is a sophisticated system of parts with an important function.

But it's harder than this, right? Because, in this case, the reader who just analyzed Simon's text is not "every reader." The reader (me) who did this analysis owns a collection of Seymour Simon's books and has closely read hundreds of informational texts. This reader has extensive background knowledge about the purposes, structures, language choices, and the types of details informational text authors use to convey ideas. This reader knows what vocabulary words such as *column, fastened, bead,* and *spool of thread* mean and has some background knowledge about the skeleton. And, not to be taken for granted, this reader is motivated to understand the text.

Hosting learning spaces where students become proficient at reading these texts is a daunting endeavor, but not an insurmountable one. This is especially true if we, as educators, understand the complexity of informational texts in general, as well as what might make a text complex for particular readers. We have to follow by teaching in a way that has generative value, coaching our students at their points of need.

So, what are the implications for our daily practice?

Let's consider your own experience as you read Simon's text and then thought through my analysis of it. Did your understanding and recall of Simon's content expand between the beginning and end of this experience? In order to make a text's complexity visible to students, we ourselves have to understand what makes a text complex. In a sense, we must be able to diagnose the complexity of a text while planning to teach and in the moment of teaching.

As educators, we also need to consider whether the tasks we assign students really help them understand how to grapple with complex texts. Many traditionally assigned tasks take for granted what the reader must do to read and learn from a text. When we ask students to write what they know about a topic, what they want to know, and what they learned, we are assuming that these students understand the content (and just need help categorizing it). What if they do not? Locating and writing answers to questions in a text also assume a certain capacity for grappling with content in a text and how the content is presented. Making connections and asking questions will not get you far in retaining the details in Simon's text if you do not also grasp his logic and attention to detail.

In addition, we need to consider whether our scaffolding is imparting too much of the content students must learn. Sometimes we do so much preteaching that students can complete the "after-reading" tasks without ever having read the text. I understand that students need to have some background or prior knowledge in order to grasp the content of the text better. Sometimes, though, I think we provide too much. We "overpreview" the text, leaving very little for the students to grapple with while reading.

Spending more time talking about the text (and completing tasks related to it) than actively reading the text means that students are not engaging directly with the author's work. This is another area of our practice we may need to reconsider. While I was writing this book, I was volunteering in my daughter's fifth-grade classroom, teaching an informational text reading workshop. The goal I worked toward intentionally was for students to spend at least half or more of a 40-minute period just reading complex (as well as stimulating) informational texts. Of course, it was difficult to squeeze in this much reading time! Frequently, by the time we factor in "before" and "after" reading exercises, there is not much time left to read. But without extensive experiences engaged in reading informational texts (with support as needed), our students cannot begin to master understanding how these texts work.

The ultimate implication for our practice is that students need numerous, productive opportunities to actively read informational texts. They need space and time to engage with more and more rigorous content as they become familiar with how these texts work. We need to be the coaches on hand for these experiences, knowledgeable about what makes texts complex and how to unpack this complexity for students. We have to be fully present, stepping in and then

stepping back in a way that keeps *learning from the text* at the center of the experience. There is a lot of power in this context for learning for every reader.

So, how do we do this?

The focus of my first book, *Close Reading of Informational Texts: Assessment-Driven Instruction in Grades 3–8* (Cummins, 2013), is primarily on instruction and on using the teaching–learning cycle to move students forward. Along with sample lessons and student work samples, teaching the following strategies is described in consecutive chapters:

- Synthesis of the ideas in informational texts.
- Analysis of the content in features and how the features support the running or main text.
- Previewing a text systematically to identify the author's purpose and make an informed prediction.
- Self-monitoring.
- Determining what is important.
- How to synthesize important information across multiple texts.

In the book you are now reading, the focus shifts from students learning with informational texts to the texts themselves. My primary goal is to affirm and stretch our awareness of what makes informational texts complex for second-through eighth-grade readers. In particular, I focus on the complexities of the extended prose in informational texts because this area is where I see many students struggling the most. Have you observed this, too? Students avoid reading and then rereading the running text, or they read it but do not grasp much more than the gist or topic of the text to share afterward. Even our advanced students who can list everything they read in a text cannot always discuss *how* the author developed his or her ideas.

In Chapter One, I define the term *text complexity* and in Chapter Two I explore the various dimensions of informational texts that contribute to their complexity for particular readers. In the following chapters, I unpack further specific dimensions. Numerous excerpts from informational texts, such as Simon's (2000) *Bones: Our Skeletal System*, are examined. Many of these texts, or parts of them, are accessible online through their publishers; I have included links (if available) to access these texts when I think viewing them might be helpful to support understanding of my analysis of their complexity. Included are texts that would be appropriate for the content areas of English language arts, science, and social studies. I am not assuming you will teach with these texts, just that these texts are similar to those you probably have access to in your classroom, school, public library, or online. Also note that the aspects of the texts I describe can cross formats; for example, although I may be discussing the types of details in an excerpt from a chapter book, the points I make about the details could also be relevant to shorter texts written in different formats (e.g., a feature article on a science news website).

Dispersed throughout this book are instructional anecdotes and samples of student work I have collected from numerous lessons in schools. I am forever grateful to the teachers who opened their classroom doors to let me "try out" some new thinking on my part. As you read descriptions of lessons, you will notice a constructivist approach to teaching. I think it is more powerful when students discover for themselves the complexities of a text. My role is to help them *notice* how texts work and then *name* what they are noticing. I strive (not always gracefully) toward having each student develop an identity as a strategic reader of informational text and gain a sense of agency, a sense of "I can do this" as he or she engages with increasingly complex texts.

Peter Johnston's (2004) book *Choice Words: How Our Language Affects Children's Learning* heavily influences my work with students in reading informational texts. Johnston's central idea is that it is a teacher's language that impacts student learning the most. The instructional recommendations I make in this book are (mostly) not about additional lessons or more to do in the short time we have with students. Instead my suggestions focus on how to integrate the language of informational text complexity into what we are already doing with students—into our modeling, our discussion of texts read aloud, and our small-group conversations and individual conferences.

Please be aware, too, that I write from the perspective of a literacy educator. What I mean is that I have read and analyzed these texts with a focus on what makes them difficult for "readers." I have not analyzed texts with a disciplinary view; in other words, I am not thinking about how to read these texts as a historian or scientist. I am assuming that opportunities to grapple with informational texts are happening as part of a larger integrated unit of study wherein meaningful, content-related thinking and learning take place. If units of study are not manageable in your classroom context, then consider how the knowledge shared in this book can be used as part of an informational text reading workshop, author study, guided reading instruction with small groups, or independent reading.

Finally, this book is an artifact of my own inquiry into what makes informational text complex and how I can reveal this complexity to students. I consider you, the reader, to be a colleague and a co-learner engaged in a similar inquiry and ready for conversation. And so, as I share my analysis of texts and my work with students, please push back at my ideas. Where is the resonance for you? Where is the dissonance? How is your knowledge of the complexity of informational texts affirmed? And how is this knowledge evolving? What instructional changes are emerging in your practices as a result? And, together, what do we need to consider next?

CHAPTER ONE

What Do We Mean by Text Complexity?

What makes an informational text complex? According to *Merriam-Webster.com* (n.d.), the word *complex* is defined as "composed of two or more parts" (*adjective*) or "a whole made up of complicated or interrelated parts" (*noun*). In the same source, the word *part* is defined as the following:

> (1) one of the often indefinite or unequal subdivisions into which something is or is regarded as divided and which together constitute the whole; (2) an essential portion or integral element.

If we think about how these definitions apply to informational texts, then we might define *text complexity* as the following:

> The quality of a text being composed of complicated or interrelated parts (one of which is the reader) that, although indefinite or unequal, are each an essential element of the whole text.

With this definition in mind, let's consider a text written for a middle school audience: *Trapped: How the World Rescued 33 Miners from 2,000 Feet Below the Chilean Desert* (Aronson, 2011). (An excerpt from the beginning of this book can be viewed at *www.simonandschuster.com/kids*. Just search the title.) One of Aronson's *purposes* in this book is to discuss the history and creation of mines. Another purpose is to recount the experiences of the miners who were trapped and then rescued and the rescue workers who endeavored to dig through solid rock hundreds of feet below ground. The overarching structure of the text is a blend of *enumerative* and *narrative* structures. (Text structures are described and explained in more detail in Chapter Four.) To draw the reader's interest, the author begins with a short narrative about the first hair-raising moments of this devastating experience. From there, he departs from the narrative to describe the geographical conditions that lead to the existence of these vast spaces deep below the Earth's surface where mining takes place. He includes *photographs* and *diagrams* that illustrate the movement of the tectonic plates and the layout and design of mines. Next he turns to the ancient history of mines, drawing from myths about Hephaistos, the Greek "god of the forge—the master of metal and fire," (p. 17) and from historical primary sources that detail mining and metal-work, including more images.

The author accomplishes all this in the first 21 pages, before he launches into an extended narrative of the miners' experience. Each "part" in Aronson's text—his purposes, his choice of structure, the text features, the content that serves as a background to the narrative (and additional parts not described here)—plays a role in building the reader's understanding of the text's central ideas. These parts do not work in isolation; instead, they come together in a larger tapestry of meaning, and these parts all contribute to the complexity of this text.

Even in texts for young readers, there are many interrelated parts that make up the whole of each text. In *Giant Pacific Octopus: The World's Largest Octopus* (Gray, 2013), the author's *purpose* is to describe this interesting species. (This first part of this book including the two pages described below can be viewed at *www.bearportpublishing.com*. Just search the title.) On the first two-page layout (pp. 4-5), the author's main idea is that the giant Pacific octopus is a large animal. There is a subheading at the top of the first page in the spread, "Giant Octopus." The *running text* (about 40 words) describes the size of the octopus with details such as "each arm can grow up to 16 feet long" (p. 4). An *illustration* compares the length of an octopus "with its arms outstretched" to the length of a minivan. On the second page, a *photograph* of an octopus with a diver nearby reveals how much smaller humans are compared with this species. There are many "parts" on this two-page spread, and each works together to convey the author's idea that the giant octopus is indeed gigantic!

So far I have only begun to explore the parts in these texts. In both Aronson's and Gray's texts, there are additional, less visibly distinct parts such as domain-specific vocabulary, varying sentence complexity, and language choices. Each of these elements (and more) contributes to the overall complexity. An equally important part of the text is the reader. The reader's life experiences, prior knowl-edge of the topic and related vocabulary, and understanding of how these texts work all contribute to the complexity of a text. In the seminal book *Teaching Reading Comprehension*, Pearson and Johnson (1978) state what we still know to be true:

Hence, one cannot know how difficult a text will be until and unless one knows something about the linguistic and conceptual sophistication of the reader: one person's *Scientific American* is another person's daily newspaper. (p. 10)

A proficient middle school reader can breeze through *Giant Pacific Octopus* (Gray, 2013) because she has read so many simple informational texts like this one. Yet she may have to slow down and read more carefully Aronson's (2011) description of how the movement of the Nazca Plate against the continent of South America contributes to the development of open spaces (cracks) deep under the earth where precious minerals are exposed. This is especially true if the reader has limited background knowledge on this topic. The many parts on the two-page spread in *Giant Pacific Octopus* may overwhelm an early or transitional reader who has not read many texts about animals or has little knowledge about the octopus. With coaching, she may begin to see how the parts are interconnected. If, on the other hand, she already knows a great deal about octopi, she may quickly recognize how each of the parts of this spread contributes to what she already knows.

The reader's purpose for reading (including reading to complete tasks assigned by the teacher) also plays a part in the complexity of a text. Tasks can make a text more complex. For example, I recently used the article "Active Earth" (Geiger, 2010) with a class of fifth graders. One group with which I worked was able to easily summarize the content after reading the article. Given the task assigned, this was a less complex text. However, when I asked them to articulate how the author *developed* the main idea in the text, they were less at ease. The nature of the task clearly made the text more complex.

The coordination and relationship of a text's many "parts," including the reader and the reader's purpose or task, is what makes an informational text complex. Why is any of this important to consider? The enhanced role given to informational texts in the Common Core State Standards (CCSS) is well known, and currently much discussion focuses on Reading Anchor Standard 10—Range of Reading and Level of Text Complexity. For both the K–5 and 6–12 strands, this anchor standard requires that students learn to "read and comprehend complex literary and informational texts independently and proficiently" (CCSSI; National Governors Association Center for Best Practices and Council of Chief State School Officers [NGA & CCSSO], 2010). Within the Reading Standards for Informational Text, Standard 10 defines a "staircase" of increasing text complexity as students move from grade to grade. The CCSS consider grades 2 and 3 to make up one "text complexity band," with grades 4 and 5 and 6 through 8 making up the next two bands. A clear message behind Standard 10 is that students should be reading more complex texts, and more and more independently, as they proceed through the grades. What is unclear in the CCSS is just what makes texts *complex* as well as what makes texts *increasingly complex*.

In an attempt to provide clarity, the authors of the CCSS present "A Three-Part Model for Measuring Text Complexity" in Appendix A (NGA & CCSSO, 2010, p. 4). This model includes examining the qualitative and quantitative dimensions of a text's complexity, as well as the reader and the task. However, explanations of the four qualitative measures of informational text complexity (levels of purpose, structure, language conventionality and clarity, and knowledge demands) are general and even vague (Fang & Pace, 2013; Hiebert & Mesmer, 2013). For example, the following statement in Appendix A (NGA & CCSSO, 2010) is from an explanation of complex versus simple structures:

> Simple informational texts are likely not to deviate from the conventions of common genres and subgenres while, complex informational texts are more likely to conform to the norms of conventions of a specific discipline. (p. 5)

In this explanation, there is little help for educators engaged in day-to-day planning with specific texts and particular readers. (I attempt to shed some light on the qualitative measures of text complexity in the following chapters.)

Following this explanation of the *qualitative* dimensions, CCSS Appendix A describes several tools for *quantitative* analysis, then briefly discusses the reader and task variables that contribute to a text's complexity. As with the explanation of the qualitative measures, the information presented on reader–task variables is general and not especially helpful. The description of the quantitative measures, though, is more concrete and accessible, including specific tools for quantitative text analysis such as the Lexile Framework for Reading, developed by MetaMetrics, Inc., and a chart (on p. 8) titled "Text Complexity Grade Bands and Associated Lexile Ranges (in Lexiles)." Teachers need only look at the bands in the chart to see where a particular student should be reading and then go to *Lexile.com* to find the Lexile level of the text they might use with this student. The result of these vague descriptions of qualitative and reader–task measures and more accessible descriptions of quantitative measures is that many policymakers and educators may put more weight on the quantitative measurement of a text's complexity (Hiebert & Mesmer, 2013).

This outcome is problematic in several ways, starting with the lack of research that supports the Lexile ranges (450–790) aligned to the text complexity band for grades 2 and 3 (Hiebert & Mesmer, 2013). The problem, according to Hiebert and Mesmer, is that this "stretch" Lexile band is "aspirational" (p. 47) and not based on empirical evidence for what is developmentally appropriate text in second and third grades. In Appendix A, the CCSS authors state, "Despite steady or growing demand from various resources, K–12 reading texts have actually trended downward in difficulty in the last half century" (NGA & CCSSO, 2010, p. 3). What the authors imply is that there is a need to increase the complexity of the texts students are reading. Hiebert & Mesmer (2013, pp. 46–47) make the case that the research cited by the CCSS authors does support this trend for the upper grades, particularly for high school texts, but not for second and third grades. In fact, texts developed for students in these grades have become more difficult in the last half century. So increasing or "stretching" the Lexile levels of texts for these readers, who have already been grappling with harder texts, does not make sense.

Emphasizing the use of quantitative measures to determine a text's complexity also limits complexity to a few "parts," such as the number of words in a text, the complexity of the sentences, and the presence of challenging vocabulary. Why is this a problem? Let's compare the Lexile level for two informational texts. The first is Nic Bishop's (2007) *Spiders*. Bishop's purpose is to describe spiders' physical attributes and behaviors. Although the text has challenging vocabulary, such as "tarantulas," "abdomen," and "camouflaged," the running text and photographs (for which Bishop is notable) scaffold understanding of these words for younger students. It is developmentally appropriate to be read aloud to students in the primary grades or to be read independently by second or third graders who are reading at transitional to early-fluent reading levels. The publisher, Scholastic, lists this book as appropriate for preschool through third grade (Scholastic, 2014). According to *Lexile.com*, the Lexile for *Spiders* is 820 (Metametrics, Inc., 2014a).

Now let's consider another text about spiders, *Stronger Than Steel: Spider Silk DNA and the Quest for Better Bulletproof Vests, Sutures, and Parachute Rope* (Heos, 2013), which is a book in the Houghton Mifflin *Scientists in the Field* series. The author's purpose in the book is to explain how a team of scientists is genetically implanting goats with the DNA of a spider called the golden orb weaver. The milk from these goats, as a result, contains proteins that can be spun into an amazingly durable silk. With an audience of middle school to early high school readers in mind, Heos reports on the concepts of DNA and genes, on different golden orb weavers and the properties of their silk, on the "spider goats" involved in the experiments, and on the team of scientists and how they go about doing this work. Just from my description of these two authors' purposes, you can surmise the difference in the complexity of Heos's text. The publisher, Houghton Mifflin, lists this book as appropriate for grades 7–10 (Houghton Mifflin Harcourt, 2013). And yet the Lexile for *Stronger Than Steel* is 860 (Metametrics, Inc., 2014b), not a significant increase in difficulty from that of the much simpler text, *Spiders*, at 820. This contrast is not simply a "blip" on the part of *Lexile.com* but a reverberating problem when looking at quantitative analyses to consider whether informational texts are appropriate for particular readers. This point reinforces the idea that *content* also contributes to the complexity of texts.

The problems described here do not mean that we should disregard the quantitative measures of a text's complexity. Nor do they mean that we should not consider important the "Three-Part Model for Measuring Text Complexity" in CCSS Appendix A (CCSSI, 2010). Both the three-part graphic of the model (p. 4) and the language of the text describing the three dimensions of text complexity advocate for "balance" (p. 7) in the implementation of the measures. However, these problems do create an imperative for educators to improve their understanding of both the qualitative dimensions of a text and of how the reader and task contribute to the text's complexity. The major focus of this book is to unpack these qualitative dimensions—to explore and begin to articulate more clearly for ourselves what makes a piece of informational text complex. While the reader–task dimension is not a major focus of this book, knowing a text well—that is, understanding the complexity of a text qualitatively—can support us in matching particular readers and specific tasks to texts.

CHAPTER TWO

What Makes an Informational Text Complex?

The qualitative dimensions of text complexity can be grouped into the following categories:

- Purpose and main ideas.
- Structure.
- Styles of language and types of vocabulary.
- Knowledge demands.

These categories were designated on the basis of my interpretation of the qualitative measures of text complexity listed in the Common Core State Standards (NGA & CCSSO, 2010), my own analysis of informational texts accessible to students in second- through eighth-grade classrooms, and my experiences working with these students. Beyond the dimensions described in this and the following chapters, there are even more that factor into the complexity of the wide range of texts we classify as "informational." The endeavor here is to continue deepening our understanding of several features that contribute to an informational text's complexity.

Purpose and Ideas

Author's Purpose

The definition of the term *purpose* is "the reason why something is done; the aim or intention of something" (*Merriam-Webster.com*, n.d.). An author has a reason why he or she is writing a text—a purpose. Traditionally, authors' purposes for writing informational texts have been placed in five categories:

1. To instruct.
2. To recount.
3. To explain.
4. To describe.
5. To persuade.

These categories are considered *genres* of informational texts. Some authors have a clear purpose that fits into one genre or another of informational text. For example, in the text *What Bluebirds Do* (Kirby, 2009) the author's purpose is to describe the behavior of a pair of bluebirds who are mating and parenting. Other authors have multiple purposes for one text, making it a blend or composite of genres. In *Bootleg: Murder, Moonshine, and the Lawless Years of Prohibition* (Blumenthal, 2011), the author's purpose is to recount the events that led up to the passage of the Eighteenth Amendment and then to its repeal. An additional purpose is to explain the numerous factors involved in both the passage and repeal of the amendment.

When trying to unpack complex texts, it is important to consider the author's purpose. A well-written text reveals a clear purpose. Still, if the purpose is not clearly stated, intermediate and middle grade readers need to be cognizant of the idea that an author *has* a purpose, and the reader may need to infer it by asking questions such as "What is the author trying to do here? Recount? Explain? Describe? Persuade?" Understanding an author's purpose moves a reader forward in recognizing structures, grasping specific content, and synthesizing the main ideas in a text. An author's purpose is discussed in more detail in Chapter Three.

Author's Main Ideas

The author's purpose is different from his or her *main idea(s)*. Before a text is even written, the author sets a purpose for writing it. The author's purpose, then, is separate from the messages interpreted by a reader who brings to the text her life experiences, prior knowledge, and so forth. In other words, the author's main ideas emerge as the reader makes sense of the text.

The meaning of the term *main idea* is sometimes elusive because educators and students have interpreted it in many ways. In this book, *main idea* (considered synonymous with "central idea") is defined as the gist or theme of an informational text. Below I discuss the difference between *gist* and *theme* and provide examples from *What Bluebirds Do* (Kirby, 2009) and *Bootleg* (Blumenthal, 2011). See Table 2.1 for a summary.

The gist of a text is a very short summary that also conveys a bigger idea or main point in the whole text or in a section of the text. The gist is specific to a particular text. For example, in *What Bluebirds Do* (Kirby, 2009), the gist is that the bluebirds have to work together to ensure the survival of their offspring. The author includes content about how the male and female bluebirds each take actions to make the nest and feed and protect their young; the reader has to infer the idea that this is "working together" and that it ensures the survival of their offspring. Essentially, the reader (with the author's purpose in mind) has to synthesize the content presented across multiple pages to come up with this gist. Understanding how the author has built this text—how this text works—aids the reader as well. Granted, some authors explicitly state the gist of a text, but when they do not, as frequently happens in texts for intermediate and middle grade readers, the reader must be fully engaged and ready to synthesize and infer.

TABLE 2.1. Purpose, Gist, and Theme

Term	Definition of term	*What Bluebirds Do* (Kirby, 2009)	*Bootleg* (Blumenthal, 2011)
Purpose	The purpose is the reason why a text is written: to provide instructions, to recount, to describe, to explain, to persuade.	The author's purpose for this text is to describe the behavior of a pair of bluebirds that is mating and parenting.	The author's purpose is to recount the events that led to the passage of the Eighteenth Amendment and then to the repeal of this amendment. An additional purpose is to explain the numerous factors involved in the passage and repeal of this amendment.
Gist	The gist of a text is a very short summary that also conveys a bigger idea or main point in the text.	One gist in this text is that the male and female bluebird mates have to work together to ensure the survival of their offspring.	One gist is that during this period, groups of activists became aware of the power of the vote and used this power as a tool for getting the Eighteenth Amendment passed in Congress.
Theme	The theme of a text is a global idea that can be applied to the text in hand.	Some species mate and work jointly to ensure the survival of their offspring.	People's beliefs drive their actions. Perseverance is required to initiate, pass, and repeal legislation. Some solutions can have unexpected effects.

In *Bootleg* (Blumenthal, 2011), one gist might be the following:

> During this period, groups of activists became aware of the power of "the vote" and used this power as a tool for getting the Eighteenth Amendment passed in Congress.

There can be more than one gist conveyed in a text. Another gist in *Bootleg* might be the following:

> The Eighteenth Amendment, which set limits on an individual's consumption of alcohol, did not necessarily have the ideal outcomes expected by its proponents. Prohibition, which led to lawlessness, corruption, murder, and social protests, could be considered a failed social experiment.

Again, identifying this gist requires active engagement by the reader, who becomes a virtual partner in conversation with the author about the text's content and the ideas being conveyed.

The theme of a text is a global idea that can be applied to both the text in hand as well as other texts. Identifying the theme is harder than identifying the gist because the reader has to think beyond the text and ask questions such as "What is the author's message in this text that I might use as a lens for under-standing other topics or issues?" Yes, the author may have a "theme" in mind while writing a text, but the reader plays a huge role in identifying this theme, using his or her real-life experiences, prior knowledge, and related vocabulary (e.g., *hope, perseverance*, and *diversity*—words not used in the text itself). A reader of *What Bluebirds Do* might derive the following idea as a theme: Some species mate and work jointly to ensure the survival of their offspring.

Again, there might be many themes in a text. The themes that emerge will depend on the reader's synthesis of the content. In *Bootleg*, the following themes might emerge:

- People's beliefs drive their actions (whether for or against some issue).
- Perseverance is required to get legislation approved or changed.
- Some solutions can have unexpected effects.

What's important to consider here is that the main ideas I have discussed (as gist or theme) are *textual*; that is, there is textual evidence to support the ideas. Most likely, the author had these ideas in mind as he or she wrote the text. With texts geared toward intermediate and middle grade students, though, there is a higher demand on readers to synthesize and infer these ideas as they read. In Chapter Eight, I explain further how main ideas are constructed.

Idea Density and Difficulty

The passage from *Bones: Our Skeletal System* (Simon, 2000) that I analyzed in the Introduction might be considered *dense* with ideas. In other words, there are a lot of ideas or details to absorb in a compact or short section of text. But the author's structuring of the text—describing the spine and then zooming from the larger backbone to the organization of the smaller vertebrae as a way to build toward a description of the spine's function—is effective. He is careful to limit the number of domain-specific terms, and he uses comparisons at critical points to promote deepening understanding. In addition, there is a full-page photograph of a section of the spine with three distinct vertebrae fastened together in a column. So although this passage is dense with ideas, Simon's intended audience (*provided* they understand how informational texts work) could make sense of what he is trying to convey. Therefore, the text is not too arduous or difficult for many well-matched readers to manage.

In some texts, though, the density of ideas can make the reading difficult, even onerous. Perhaps the author's purpose is too ambitious, and he or she wants to report too much content. It could also be possible that the author assumes, inappropriately for his or her audience, too much prior knowledge on the part of the readers. Consider this passage, which is the first paragraph in the book *England: The Land* (Banting, 2012; the words *bogs* and *moors* are bold in the original text):

> From above, England looks like a patchwork quilt made of many squares. Each square is a farmer's field, where crops such as wheat and beets grow. Between the farms are lush valleys, rolling green hills, **bogs**, **moors**, and mountains. Along with Scotland to the north and Wales to the southwest, this green land occupies the island of Great Britain. Great Britain is part of a country called the United Kingdom, which includes Northern Ireland. Northern Ireland shares an island with Republic of Ireland, to the west. (p. 4)

For the intended audience, perhaps fourth grade students and older, there is an overwhelming amount of content in this paragraph. Banting's purpose seems to be to describe the landscape and location of England. Like Simon's structure in *Bones,* but in reverse, Banting attempts to move from a close-up view of England's terrains to a wider view of its location in regard to other regions and countries. She begins with a comparison of England's landscape to a patchwork quilt and then notes the types of crops that can be grown there. Unlike Simon's solid analogy of each vertebra in the spine being "hard and hollow, like a bead or spool of thread" and the vertebrae forming "a flexible chain of bones that can twist like a string of beads" (n.p.), Banting's (2012) analogy of a patchwork quilt quickly falls apart. If each of a farmer's crop fields represents a patch on a quilt, then what do the spaces "between the farms"—"lush valleys, rolling green hills, bogs, moors, and mountains" (p. 4)—represent? The author doesn't tell us.

The passage also contains an abundant amount of vocabulary that is likely to be unfamiliar to many intermediate grade readers. What does it mean for a valley to be *lush*? What does it mean for a hill to *roll*? What are *bogs* and *moors*? It is not that these readers shouldn't read texts with these terms and learn them, but the density of terms and the lack of support in figuring them out do not make grappling with the meaning of these terms feasible.

The text becomes even more difficult in this sentence from the same passage:

> Along with Scotland to the north and Wales to the southwest, this green land occupies the island of Great Britain.

First, the text does not include a map to use as a reference. So the reader has to tap her understanding of maps and directionality and create a mental image of Scotland "to the north" and Wales "to the southwest." To the north and southwest of what, though? We do not know yet because the author does not state the subject of the sentence—"this green land" (p. 4)— until after this initial phrase. Even then the reader has to realize that the words "this green land" refer to England. "Green" is only noted as a descriptor of "hills" in the second sentence. So the reader has to infer that the author is considering all of the farmers' fields, the valleys, the hills, the bogs, and the moors to be "green" and, therefore, that "this green land" must be referring to England. Finally, returning to the mental map, the reader has to visualize Scotland, Wales, and England "occupying" the island of Great Britain.

Take a moment to reread the initial excerpt from this book again. The last two sentences could be considered misleading or just confusing. (I had to engage in a search of terms on the Internet to make sense of it all myself.) Somehow the reader has to figure out that England, "along with" Scotland and Wales, are parts of a larger region called Great Britain (which is also an island), although this is never stated directly. Great Britain and Northern Ireland are two regions that, combined, make up the country, or sovereign state, called the "United Kingdom." (Technically, the name of this country is the United Kingdom of Great Britain and Northern Ireland.) The rest of Ireland (separate from Northern Ireland, but still the same island) is its own sovereign state, called the "Republic of Ireland."

By now the difficulty of this text should be clear, so I will just add that there are no maps featured on this page or the next facing page. There are four photographs on these two pages, but they are of little help in understanding the text. The second and only other paragraph on the page is equally dense and difficult.

Yes, this is only the first page of a book about England, but even as an introduction it is unreasonably dense and conceptually difficult, with some problematic gaps in the content. Reading and understanding this text was arduous, even for me. Sometimes a text's complexity is appropriate and provides an opportunity for a reader to engage in rigorous thinking and learning. At other times, a text is simply difficult and, as a result, unmanageable for certain readers. Frequently this occurs when the ideas are too dense because the author is covering too much content and assuming too much knowledge on the reader's part. It might also just be that the text is badly written.

Structure

According to *Merriam-Webster.com* (n.d.), the definition of the term *structure* is "the way that something is built, arranged, or organized." This definition implies that the parts serve to support each other or are interrelated. An author's purpose governs how he or she structures a text. In other words, the author constructs a text, arranging and organizing its parts, with the purpose of the text in mind. This carefully built, purpose-driven structure contributes to the cohesion of a text, the unity of ideas. The more cohesive a text, the more likely the reader will be able to follow the flow or logic of the author's ideas.

Traditional Structures at the Macro and Micro Levels

There are five structures commonly referred to in the professional literature:

1. Enumerative.
2. Sequence/chronology/narrative.
3. Comparison.
4. Causal relationships.
5. Problem–solution.

(See Table 2.2 for a brief explanation of these structures; they are explained in more detail in Chapter Four.)

Some authors use these structures at the *macro level*; this means that the whole text (or a large section of the text) is organized into one of these structures. In my experience, enumerative, sequence/chronology/narrative, and problem–solution structures are more often employed as whole-text structures at the macro level than is comparison or causal relationships structures. But authors also employ these structures at the *micro level*—in a sentence or just a few sentences. When an author does this, it can be considered a *type of detail* rather than a text's structure. For example, at multiple points in *Trapped*, Aronson (2011) departs from the narrative of the miner's experience to describe the equipment being used to rescue

TABLE 2.2. Brief Description of Text Structures

Type of structure	Brief description
Enumerative	The text has an overarching topic and clear subtopics that provide more information about the main topic.
Sequence/chronology/narrative	The text is written as a series of steps in a process or of events in time order.
Comparison	The content of the text examines the differences and similarities between two or more objects or ideas.
Causal relationships	The cause(s) and effect(s) of a particular situation or context are explained.
Problem–solution	A problem is identified, and a solution or possible solution is explained.

Note. See Chapter Four for an in-depth discussion regarding each of these structures.

the miners. In the following two sentences, Aronson's comparison of different drills to a percussion hammer water-well drill functions at the micro or detail level:

> Other drills cut by turning, screwing down into the ground. This percussion hammer pounds as it turns. (p. 78)

In this example, Aronson uses a comparison as a type of detail to build and convey an idea. This distinction between text structures employed by authors at the macro and micro levels is discussed further in Chapter Four.

Figurative Language and Other Types of Details

As just mentioned, authors use several types of details to build meaning in a text. These details, which exist at the micro or detail level, might occur in a few sentences, in a single sentence, or even in just a phrase. Remember my analysis in the Introduction of the excerpt from Simon's (2000) *Bones: Our Skeletal System*? To describe the backbone, he uses details about the backbone's location, its parts, and its physical attributes. He also uses similes, comparing the "hard and hollow" attributes of a vertebra to "a bead or spool of thread" (n p.). Details contribute to the structure of a text, and being able to recognize categories or types of details can help a reader begin to grasp the content. Imagine if a reader said, "Oh, Simon just named the *location* of the spine! It runs down the middle of the body!"

Similes and other types of figurative language are rampant in informational texts. Brian Floca's Caldecott Award-winning book *Locomotive* (Floca, 2013) is peppered with *onomatopoeia* describing the sounds of the train: "huffs," "bangs," "chug-chug," and "whoooooo whoooo whoo." He employs *personification* as well, clearly casting the locomotive as female: "She's waiting in the railyard, ready for her work" (n.p.). Like Simon, Floca utilizes *similes* in sentences, such as, "Up in the cab—small as a closet, hot as a kitchen—it smells of smoke, hot metal, and oil" (n.p.). He also plays with *alliteration* in his descriptions, such as the work of the steam moving the train forward: "It *pushes pushes pushes* the pistons, which *push* and *pull* the rods" (n.p.). Figurative language is part of how a text works; it plays a role in the overall structure of a text. Different types of details commonly found in non-narrative and narrative informational texts are described further in Chapters Five and Six.

Multimodality

There are multiple modes, used for a variety of purposes, in informational texts. The visual mode includes the *running text* and the *text features* and how these two aspects are designed and laid out. Online texts offer additional modes in which information can be experienced, for example, with video and audio clips. Many of these texts can be interacted with and marked up by the reader as well, thereby providing yet another way to experience the text. Multimodality contributes to the complexity of a text.

To illustrate the complexity of a multimodal text, let's consider the initial two-page spread of an online *Junior Scholastic* article titled "The Real Cost of Fashion" (Anastasia, 2013). (I recommend viewing this article—in particular the first two pages—to aid in understanding my explanation below, at *junior. scholastic.com/issues/09_02_13/book#/6*.) One of the author's purposes in this article is to describe the complex relationships between clothing manufacturers in the United States and the contractors to whom they outsource work in less industrialized nations. On the far left-hand side of the first two-page spread, the author includes a series of three different-sized photographs that convey the effects of having access to cheap clothing. The first image is of a smiling teen in a dress and heels, accessorized with sunglasses and carrying several shopping bags in both hands. Next there is a graphic arrow that draws the reader's eye up the page from the shopper to a photograph of an unsmiling Chinese female worker, sitting at a sewing machine in a long row of other employees also sitting at machines. Overlapping, just to the right, is a third photograph of the factory that collapsed in Bangladesh in the spring of 2013. A clear message is conveyed in this series of three images.

The last photograph has a graphic of a small circle with the words "watch the video." The reader can click on this circle and watch a news video describing the working conditions of these factories, the tragedy of the factory collapse, and shifts in government policy to provide more rights for workers. Here the reader experiences a message via visual and auditory modes of text.

In the bottom right-hand corner of the second page, separate from the photographs and the video icon, there is a chart with a photograph of a denim shirt in the center. On one side of the shirt are statistics outlining the cost of manufacturing this shirt in the United States and, on the other side, the (much cheaper) cost of manufacturing the same shirt in Bangladesh. This chart provides still another way to experience the author's message.

Then there is the running text with statistics and details that reveal the pros and cons for multiple issues in this context. Yes, the working conditions in these countries can be unsafe, but these are the only jobs for many poor people in those countries. Yes, the disaster was terrible and working conditions should be improved, but the cost of making and sustaining the improvements may encourage manufacturers to leave the country in search of cheaper labor. Yes, clothing manufacturers can make their products in the United States, where conditions are guaranteed to be safer, but the cost of clothing for the American consumer would go up drastically. And so forth.

Together, the series of photographs, the video, the chart, and the running text make the entire informational text *complex*. Each contributes to the meaning, but they are also carefully interwoven to create the larger meaning in the text. The result is not only multiple ways for the reader to experience the content, but also multiple layers of information that serve to reinforce, again and again, the author's main ideas.

Text Features

As noted in the discussion of multimodality, the *features* of a text also contribute to its complexity. Text features are distinguishable elements of a text. More important, they serve to interconnect the multitude of other parts in a text, helping readers access the main ideas. Think about the first three images in the *Junior Scholastic* article, "The Real Cost of Fashion" (Anastasia, 2013), I just described. This series of photos helps readers visually access the main ideas in the article. Other text features that provide similar support, or even extend the ideas in the text, include:

- Photographs and illustrations.
- Captions and labels.

- Diagrams.
- Charts and graphs.
- Tables.
- Boxes and sidebars.
- Maps.
- Glossaries and pronunciation guides.

Still other text features help the reader locate information and even predict what content will be included in the text, such as:

- Titles.
- Contents.
- Headings and subheadings.
- Index.

In the past decade, text features have become an integral part of informational texts, supporting the author's purpose, the running text, and the development of the main ideas.

Layout and Design

When I was in elementary and middle school in the mid-1970s to early 1980s, I rarely read informational texts except to write the required annual research report. This may have been because these informational texts came in just two colors: black and white. When you looked at a text, you could expect to see a lot of extended prose and a few text features interspersed here and there—a heading or subheading in a plain font, a photograph (black and white), perhaps a map or diagram or chart. The presentation was flat and dull. As you have probably noticed, texts have changed tremendously. Now they are full of eye-appealing features, sometimes too many! When we try to make sense of so many features, it is important to consider the role that layout and design plays in the structure of the text.

The layout of a text is the way in which the various parts, such as text features, extended text, key words in bold print, and so forth, are positioned on the page. The design is the purpose and planning behind the layout. Layouts are intended to be attractive and catch the reader's eye. More noteworthy, though, the layout of a page is carefully planned to serve the author's purpose and to provide a way for aspects of the text and the ideas they convey to be presented cohesively. On the two-page spread of the *Junior Scholastic* article (Anastasia, 2013) discussed previously, the intentional layout and design reveal the author's purpose and ideas. The text features I described are laid out in a way that makes accessing the purpose and predicting the main ideas feasible. For example, just as English prose is written from left to right, there is a clear left-to-right orientation in the series of three photographs, beginning at the bottom left-hand side of the first page and moving up and to the right. The chart comparing the costs of making a shirt is tucked neatly into the bottom right-hand corner of the second page. Positioning the chart this way does not interfere with the orientation and meaning of the series of photographs. After the reader has digested the first set of images, she can turn her attention to this chart without being disturbed by other graphics or images as a result of the chart's placement.

Language and Vocabulary

Register and Tone

Register, or style, is a particular type of language used for a particular purpose. The tone of the text is the way the author expresses his or her attitude throughout the text. In what we might consider traditional informational texts, the register is frequently formal and the tone is distant, unemotional, and objective. Mostly, the author is presented as the expert, imparting information to the reader. For example, the passage from *England: The Land* (Banting, 2012) discussed earlier is written in a formal register and objective tone. This style of text tends to distance the author and the reader from each other and discusses subjects in the grammatical third person as *he, she*, and *they*.

Many authors of informational texts still use the grammatical third person, but have adopted a less formal tone. A good example is *How They Croaked: The Awful Ends of the Awfully Famous* (Bragg, 2012). This passage is from a chapter titled "Elizabeth I: She Kept Her Head about Her":

> The red-haired Elizabeth was twenty-five years old when the coronation ring was placed on her long, narrow finger. Now that she was queen, her advisers set her up on dates and told her to get a husband, have an heir, and then she'd be safe. She liked men and they liked her—but she liked her head more. (p. 44)

The author employs a humorous tone and a less formal style, using colloquial language such as "told her to get a husband" and "she liked men and they liked her." His register and tone serve his purpose: to describe the gruesome deaths of famous historical figures in an entertaining way, for an audience of intermediate to middle grade students.

Heart and Soul: The Story of America and African Americans (Nelson, 2011) is a narrative told from the perspective of a fictionalized, elder African American woman. Nelson uses a grammatical first person, with the narrator fully present as "I," engaged in a conversation with the reader as "we." The woman speaks directly to the reader in an informal register with an intimate tone:

> Many of us are getting up in age and feel it's time to make some things known before they are gone for good. So it's important that you pay attention, honey, because I'm only going to tell you this story but once. (p. 7)

The narrator continues the conversation throughout the book, asking the reader questions such as "Oh, did I mention that their 'property' included us?" (p. 13). This question positions the reader as an active meaning maker who has been processing what was said prior to this point in the text. Nelson's choices of register and tone support his purpose. The result is that the reader experiences a narrative of African American history—ordinary people facing and overcoming terrible obstacles—alongside a wise elder who has experienced racial discrimination herself.

In *Things That Float and Things That Don't* (Adler, 2013), the author's purpose is to explain the properties of density—size, weight, and shape—by observing whether everyday objects sink or float. Adler speaks directly to the reader: "Why do ice and icebergs float? You can find the answer in your freezer" (n.p.). He implies that a conversation is happening between himself and the reader. He asks you, the reader, a question. Then he responds, as though in a conversation, with his own answer. Adler uses the grammatical second person ("you"), and although his style is less formal, he still positions himself as the expert or person-in-the-know.

General Academic Vocabulary

Academic vocabulary is vocabulary associated with schooling occurring relatively frequently in different classroom contexts. For example, students might hear the term *evaluation* used during the analysis of literary texts, during the discussion of a method used during a science lab, and when considering the value of including a primary source as part of a history presentation. In the case of informational texts, academic vocabulary may include terms used in the texts themselves, in a discussion of texts, and in thinking through the writing used in these kinds of texts. Students must understand an abundance of these words to work effectively with informational texts—that is, to comprehend the content and ideas and to communicate their learning. Consider the academic vocabulary already discussed in this chapter related to the types of details (*location, physical attribute, simile*), text features (*graphics, diagrams, photographs*), and text structures (*enumerative, problem–solution, causal relationships*).

In addition, there are connective words such as *however, moreover,* and *nonetheless* that reveal the relationships between ideas. Connectives create cohesion between ideas. These words are generally categorized in four groups: additive, temporal, causal, and adversative. I discuss connectives further in Chapter Seven.

Domain-Specific Vocabulary

Informational text authors rely heavily on domain-specific vocabulary to formulate and develop ideas. These are content-area words that students may not see very often when they are reading broadly but will see several times during a unit of study on a particular topic or issue. Notice the domain-specific words in this excerpt from the book *Honeybees* (Heiligman, 2002):

> Worker bees called nurse bees feed the larva royal jelly, which comes out of glands in a worker bee's head. Royal jelly is packed with vitamins and proteins. When the larva is three days old, the workers begin feeding her beebread, a mixture of honey and pollen from flowers. (p. 11)

This short paragraph is packed with domain-specific vocabulary. In the first sentence alone, Heiligman names a general type of bee—the *worker bee*—and then a more specific type of bee—the *nurse bee.* She names the food, *royal jelly*, that is fed to the *larva,* and describes where this food comes from—*glands* in the worker bee's head.

Domain-specific vocabulary is frequently considered hard for students to grasp and master. The beauty of informational texts is that these terms are frequently consistent across texts on the same topics or issues. Multiple exposures to these words while reading texts in classroom discussions and during other learning experiences will deepen students' understanding of these words.

Knowledge Demands

Authors are aware of their audience and have certain expectations about their readers' familiarity with their topics and ideas. Knowledge demands refers to expectations about readers' life experiences (background knowledge), prior knowledge, and content or disciplinary knowledge.

Background Knowledge

Students' background knowledge is the knowledge they have developed as part of life experiences outside of the school classroom. As we know, these experiences vary widely, and tapping these experiences may or may not be useful in understanding informational texts. Many authors try to help their readers use background knowledge to grapple with conceptually difficult ideas. For example, in *A Black Hole Is NOT a Hole*, DeCristofano (2012) uses snowballs as a way to think about the force of gravity:

> When there's a lot of matter, there's a strong pull. Less matter means a weaker pull. For example, imagine a fluffy snowball and a harder-packed snowball of the same size. The fluffier ball is made of less stuff. Its pull is wimpier than the pull of the densely packed ball.
>
> You can feel this difference when you hold the two snowballs in your hand. Each one presses down on your hand because of the gravitational attraction it shares with Earth. The hard-packed snowball has a stronger attraction to Earth because it is made of more material. (p. 14)[1]

The problem here is that background knowledge, or personal life experiences, are not universal. If you have lived in a place where there is enough snow to make snowballs, you can tap personal experiences to understand the text better. If you have never seen or experienced snow, this connection may not help you much.

Prior Knowledge

Prior knowledge is information or skills acquired during school experiences—formal academic or domain-specific knowledge. Sometimes authors assume a reader has particular prior knowledge. In the text *Alien Deep: Revealing the Mysterious Living World at the Bottom of the Ocean* (Hague, 2012), the author's purposes are to describe the hydrothermal vents located the bottom of the ocean and to narrate the story of a team of scientists who explored the vents. Early in the book, there is a section wherein the author describes the initial discovery of hydrothermal vents deep in the ocean. In order to understand the physical attributes of hydrothermal vents, the reader also needs to understand the role of the Earth's plate tectonics in creating those vents. In this case, Hague does not take this knowledge for granted and clearly defines and describes *plates* and *plate tectonics* in the following excerpt:

> Today, we know that Earth's crust is broken into great slabs called plates that travel across the planet's surface as though on some sort of slow-moving conveyor belt. The complex interaction of these plates is called plate tectonics, and it is the force

---

[1] From *A Black Hole Is NOT a Hole*. Text copyright © 2012 by Carolyn Cinami DeCristofano. Used by permission of Charlesbridge Publishing, Inc. All rights reserved.

behind mountain building, volcanic and earthquake activity, and the slow reshap-ing of Earth's continents. (p. 13)

In the next paragraph, however, Hague doesn't define or explain the mantle and core parts of the Earth's layers. He assumes his readers have some prior knowledge of these concepts when he writes the following:

At places where two plates were pulling apart, known as spreading centers, geolo-gists thought that heat from the mantle would break through as a sort of exhaust system for Earth's core. (p. 13)

Even in the first excerpt, when Hague states, "Today, we know that the Earth's crust is broken into great slabs," he is assuming the reader knows that the *crust* is the Earth's outermost layer.

Disciplinary Viewpoint

Another common assumption of informational text authors is that readers understand the ways of thinking and creating knowledge that are inherent to the author's field. For example, scientists and engineers engage in inquiry through *investigating, evaluating*, and developing *explanations and solutions*. This inquiry is an iterative process that also includes asking questions, observing, experiment-ing, measuring, arguing, critiquing, analyzing, imagining, reasoning, calculating and predicting. Knowledge is not treated as a static entity; instead it accumulates, changes, shifts, emerges, and evolves. This way of thinking and creating knowl-edge is inherent in texts about science and engineering; frequently, the authors are actually scientists or engineers themselves. An example of this kind of think-ing, this kind of creating knowledge, is apparent in the book just described, *Alien Deep* (Hague, 2012). The author contrasts what was understood in the field of geology in the 1970s with what we know now. He implies that arriving at our current understanding of hydrothermal vents required not only discovery, but also "finding" that discovery—that is, asking questions, inventing methods to explore, observing, and so forth (p. 13).

Authors of historical texts consult primary and secondary sources related to their topics. Their conclusions are based on their interpretation of these sources. In a sense, these authors make claims or educated guesses about their topics based on the evidence they gather from their sources. The authors' choices of language in a text reveal their interpretation. For example, in *The Dust Bowl Through the Lens* (Sandler, 2009), notice the language the author uses in the first sentence of the section called "Destroying the Land":

> Certain that wheat prices would continue to rise and confident that the beneficial rains so vital to the crops would continue to bless the region, southern plains farmers plowed up miles of the virgin prairie soil. (p. 10)

Words such as "certain" and "confident" have an evaluative connotation. Sandler has made a judgment about the mindset of the farmers, based on his research and interpretation of sources. It's not that most of us are not in agreement with the author. As readers, we just need to realize that his account of what happened and the motivation and mindset of the agents involved are the author's interpretation.

An abbreviated description of each of the qualitative dimensions I described in this chapter can be found in the last part of the book, "Closing Thoughts," Table 1, pp. 126–129. In the next six chapters, I examine in more detail five of the qualitative dimensions of text complexity introduced in this chapter:

1. Author's purpose.
2. Text structure.
3. Types of details (in non-narrative and narrative texts).
4. Connectives.
5. Main idea construction.

Although these chapters discuss in isolation particular qualitative dimensions of informational text, we need to remember that these *parts* are connected and contribute to the *whole*.

CHAPTER THREE

What Do We Mean
by an Author's Purpose?

As stated in the previous chapter, the definition of the term *purpose* is "the reason why something is done; the aim or intention of something." The purpose of a text is usually determined before the writing begins, while the main ideas emerge as the text is developed and as the reader makes meaning of the content. If the author's purpose is not explicitly stated, the reader may have to infer it. For informational texts, purposes generally fit into the following five genres:

1. To instruct.
2. To recount.
3. To explain.
4. To describe.
5. To persuade.

These genres provide the language a reader needs to articulate the author's purpose. While I have identified these five genres in particular, this list is by no means complete. Some teachers have asked me about purposes such as *to entertain* or *to inspire*. If students can make the argument using textual evidence that this is the author's purpose, then, fine! Add it to the list you have created for your class or make it a subcategory of one of these genres. The important point is to use the *language of genres* to describe what we understand about *how texts work*. Table 3.1 summarizes the five genres of purpose explored in this chapter in "kid-friendly" language.

In this book I distinguish informational *genres* as different from *forms* or *formats* of informational writing, such as picture books, graphic novels, brochures,

TABLE 3.1. "Kid-Friendly" Definitions of Author's Purposes

Purpose	Definition
Instruct	The author wants to provide instructions for the reader to be able to do something. Example: In *Look Up! Bird-Watching in Your Own Backyard* (Cate, 2013), the author provides instructions for how to watch birds.
Recount	The author wants to tell a reader what happened, tell about a past experience, or tell the story of a particular group or event. Example: In *The Great Fire* (Murphy, 2010), the author's purpose is to recount the events just before, during, and after the fire of 1871 that destroyed much of Chicago.
Explain	The author wants to make clear how something works, how something is produced, or why something occurs or occurred. Examples: In *Toilet: How It Works* (Macaulay, 2013), the author's purpose is to explain how waste disposal works. In *Titanic: Voices from the Disaster* (Hopkinson, 2012), one of the author's purposes is to explain the many factors that contributed to the death of so many passengers.
Describe	The author wants to report on, or describe, the attributes, properties, and behaviors of a thing, or class, or group of things, or a particular context. Example: In *Rocks and Minerals* (Symes, 1988), the author describes different types of rocks, such as igneous and volcanic rocks.
Persuade	The author wants to persuade you to do or believe something. This genre includes writing opinions and arguments. Example: In *Waste and Recycling* (Hewitt, 2009), the author wants to talk you into reusing or recycling materials so they do not end up in landfills.

Suggestion: I recommend replacing the examples of specific texts (as needed) with developmentally appropriate texts for your students, texts you have used during instruction, or texts relevant to your units of study. For this part, you might also consider engaging in shared writing after reading a text that fits in a particular structure.

and news articles. Different forms of informational writing might fit into the same genre. Both the graphic novel *The 9/11 Report* (Jacobson & Colon, 2006) and the chapter book *Blizzard of Glass: The Halifax Explosion of 1917* (Walker, 2011) are narratives recounting harrowing experiences in American history. The authors' forms of writing differ, though. In *Planet Earth Scrapbook: Amazing Animals of the Rainforest* (West, 2009), the author's purpose is to describe rainforests. West's layout and design resemble a scrapbook with photographs and separate boxes featuring non-narrative text on several different subtopics. In *Animal Poems of the Iguazú* (Alarcón, 2008), the author's purpose is also to describe a rainforest, specifically the Iguazú Falls in Argentina. Unlike West's scrapbook-like format, though, Alarcon's format is poetry.

An author can also have more than one purpose, making the text a blend or composite of genres. In *The Elephant Scientist* (O'Connell & Jackson, 2011) one of the authors' purposes is to recount the events of a research expedition to observe elephant herds in Etosha National Park. Another purpose is to describe the physical attributes and behaviors of elephants, and yet another purpose is to explain the communication between elephant herds (that was discovered during the expedition).

In the rest of this chapter, I describe each of the genres of informational text I've noted. Please keep in mind that my objective is to provide language we can use to articulate an author's purpose. Whereas many texts lend themselves to easy identification of the author's purpose(s) or genre(s), some texts may be more challenging. The point is not to "nail" a genre to a text, but to use the concept of genre and the language that we attribute to particular genres to help us articulate the author's purpose(s) and progress in our understanding.

To Instruct

One purpose for a text is to provide instructions in a way that enables a reader to engage in a particular experience or activity. For example, in *Look Up! Bird-Watching in Your Own Backyard* (Cate, 2013), the author's purpose is to instruct the reader on how to watch birds by providing general guidelines. Cate, the author, makes suggestions for how you can bird-watch anywhere, including your backyard, and provides guidance for how to identify birds by color, shape, and sound. (Sample pages from this text can be viewed at *www.candlewick.com*. Just search the title at this site.) *Procedures* are types of instructions that provide specific steps (rather than general suggestions or guidelines) for doing something. In the text *How to Make Bubbles* (Shores, 2011), for example, the author's purpose is to enable the reader to produce thin spheres of liquid soap that float. Each page contains one clear step in the procedure.

Why are instructions the purpose of a text and not part of the text's *structure*? Although Cate's purpose in *Look Up!* (2013) is to instruct, her text structure is enumerative. She introduces her topic, bird-watching, and then moves to a discussion of numerous aspects of bird-watching. Each of these subtopics has instructional implications for the reader; the structure she has chosen serves her purpose. By contrast, in *How to Make Bubbles* (2011), Shores has chosen a sequence text structure that includes a materials list, specific steps written as imperatives (e.g., "Add 1 cup of dish soap"), and photographs that show a child completing a step. Although both authors have a similar purpose, their structures are very different. I discuss enumerative and other types of text structures in Chapter Four.

The main ideas a reader gleans from each of these texts differ as well. In *Look Up!* (Cate, 2013) one of the main ideas is that you, the reader, can watch birds anywhere, with whatever you already have on hand, whenever you have time. In *How to Make Bubbles* (Shores, 2011), a main idea is that the reader needs to have particular materials and follow specific steps to make bubbles.

To Recount

When an author's purpose is to recount, he or she wants to do one or more of the following:

- Tell a reader what happened.
- Tell about a past experience.
- Tell the story of a particular group or event.

In *The Great Fire* (Murphy, 2010) one of the author's purposes is to recount the events just before, during, and after the fire of 1871 that destroyed much of Chicago. Like many informational texts for intermediate and middle grade students, though, Murphy's text is more complex than a simple narrative structure. He has purposes beyond recounting. He explains the many flaws in Chicago's emergency plan that led to even more devastation. These explanations are integrated into the narrative structure of the text making this a blend of genres. In a final chapter, entitled "Myth and Reality," he also attempts to persuade the reader to question certain myths about the fire.

In *The Many Faces of George Washington: Remaking a Presidential Icon* (McClafferty, 2011) one of the author's purposes is to recount how a team of specialists—historians, experts in developing computerized 3-D models, sculptors, make-up artists, wig makers, and more—endeavored to create accurate, life-size representations of George Washington at three pivotal points in his life. A second purpose of the book is to recount the life experiences of Washington during these times. (You can view sample pages from this book at *www.lernerbooks. com.* Just search the title.)

Although both Murphy and McClafferty's texts fall into the recount genre, their structures differ. Murphy's text is written as a narrative, in a temporal order, whereas McClafferty's text is enumerative in structure for the first three chapters. Then the rest of the book alternates between the narrative of the team's endeavor and the narrative of George Washington's life.

The first three chapters describe and set the context for both narratives. At George Washington's Mount Vernon Estate and Gardens, a popular tourist site, the Mount Vernon Ladies' Association, which owns and maintains the site, and James Rees, the president of the site, have researched Americans' perceptions of the first U.S. president and realized that most Americans associate him with the stodgy old man in the portrait on the one dollar bill. Given the tremendous amount of evidence that this portrait is inaccurate, the leadership wanted to change Americans' perceptions of what George Washington looked like. In addition to introducing this issue, McClafferty describes more accurate historical representations and images of Washington that still exist, including a plaster mask and full body statue of Washington made by a Parisian artist. The author introduces the reader to modern technology that can be used to create more accurate pictures of what Washington looked like, based on the historical evidence.

Beginning with the fourth and fifth chapters, McClafferty alternates between the purposes of recounting the experiences of George at ages 11–20, 45, and 57, and the experiences of the team of specialists. For example, in Chapter Four, "Becoming Washington," the author's purpose is to recount episodes from Washington's youth and young adulthood. During this period, Washington was hopeful about the future of the colonies and still loyal to Britain. He was a surveyor and then, after his brother's death, began his military career and defended Britain's interests against France. He quickly became a reliable member of the militia, even a leader. In Chapter Five, "Washington at Nineteen," McClafferty pauses her narrative about Washington's early adulthood to describe how the specialist team went about creating a statue of Washington in his youth. The work included scanning his dentures (available in the collection of artifacts at Mt. Vernon) and combining these images with images of another man's jawbone—that of a man who lived in the same time period and was similar in size to Washington. Here the author demonstrates an additional purpose of explaining how modern technology can be used to recreate life-like images of historical figures.

In the next four chapters, McClafferty continues to alternate between these two narratives, examining two more periods of Washington's life (ages 45 and 57). She closes with a final chapter summarizing the efforts of the specialists and the effect these representations of Washington may have on visitors to Mt. Vernon.

In summary, we can see that although recounting is one purpose of both Murphy's and McClafferty's texts, both authors reveal additional purposes for writing these books and use different text structures as well.

To Explain

When an author's purpose is to explain, he or she wants to make clear how something works, how something is produced, or why something occurs. It is important to note that an explanation is focused on the *process*, on what happens when a group of factors interact, not on the end product or on a particular event. An explanation answers questions such as:

- How does something work? How is something produced? What is the process?
- Why did an event happen? What factors contributed to the occurrence of this event?
- How did something come to be, and why does it persist?

In *Toilet: How It Works* (Macaulay, 2013) the author's purpose is to explain how waste disposal operates. His text structure is the sequential steps in the process, beginning with pushing the handle on the toilet all the way through the final step when the treatment plant releases clean water into a nearby river.

In *Titanic: Voices from the Disaster* (Hopkinson, 2012) the author's purpose is not only to tell the story of this tragedy, but to explain the many factors that contributed to the sinking of the ship and the loss of so many lives. This purpose is made clear in a series of sidebars with subtitles such as "WHY WEREN'T THERE ENOUGH LIFEBOATS?" (p. 32). In one sidebar titled "THE *TITANIC*'S WATERTIGHT DOORS" (p. 88), the author first describes these doors and then asks, "So why didn't the *Titanic*'s watertight doors keep the ship from sinking?" explicitly revealing her purpose.

Hopkinson's structure is intricate. She has an overarching or macro-level chronological structure focused on major moments in this tragedy: a peaceful first day at sea, the initial impact when the ship hit the iceberg, and so forth. Tightly threaded into this structure are the stories of dozens of crew members and all classes of passengers along with vivid descriptions of the ship's many amenities and engineering advances, as well as the food, the music, and the weather. The sidebars just mentioned also have a cause and (implied) effect structure. This blend of structures serves the purposes of the text: recounting the events of this tragedy and explaining why it happened.

In *The Case of the Vanishing Golden Frogs: A Scientific Mystery* (Markle, 2012) the author's purpose is to explain why the Panamanian golden frog, the national symbol of Panama, is disappearing from the wild. (You can view pages from this book at *www.lernerbooks.com*. Just search by title.) Markle uses one scientist's investigation over time as the macro structure for the text, chronicling how Karen Lips (along with other scientists) observed the frogs, asked many questions, pursued several possible answers, and then discovered the cause of the frogs' deaths. As a result of this research, Project Golden Frog was established in order to gather and raise healthy frogs in isolated environments. As you can see, this text is also written in a problem–solution text structure. I discuss this issue further in Chapter Four.

Notice that each of these authors has a purpose of explaining something. Macaulay is explaining a linear process. Hopkinson is explaining how many factors contributed to a tragic event. Markle is explaining how the genesis of a problem can be discovered and addressed. Notice also that the structure of these texts varies, reinforcing the point that we need to consider an author's purpose *before* analyzing a text's structure because, in the end, the purpose drives the development of the structure.

To Describe

When an author wants to describe the attributes, properties, and behaviors of a thing or a group of things, or a particular context, this purpose falls into the genre of description. Simon's (2000) purpose in *Bones: Our Skeletal System* is to report on, or describe, the bones or groups of bones that make up parts of our skeletal system. The purpose of the popular *DK Eyewitness Books* is to describe particular topics. For example, in *Rocks and Minerals* (Symes, 1988), the author describes different types of rocks, such as igneous and volcanic. His purpose also is to explain how rocks are formed. So this particular book is a composite of genres.

In Scholastic's humor-filled *You Wouldn't Want to . . .* series, each author has a descriptive purpose. In *You Wouldn't Want to Be Sick in the 16th Century: Diseases You'd Rather Not Catch*, Senior (2014) describes the practices of doctors in that period, the people who could and could not afford services, and some of the terrible deaths that occurred because so little was known about medicine at that time.

Written in a question-answer format, titles from the Sterling Children's Books *Good Question!* series are composites of two genres, description and explanation. For example, in *How Does the Ear Hear? And Other Questions About the Five Senses* (Stewart, 2014), the author describes the senses, the parts of the body related to the senses, and all the things you can do with your senses. She also explains how the senses work, as when "sound waves crash into your eardrum" (p. 15), starting a causal chain that eventually leads to signals being sent to the brain.

To Persuade

When an author's purpose is to persuade a reader, he or she wants to influence the reader to do or believe something. This is perhaps the hardest genre to identify. Some authors, particularly in shorter texts formatted as essays or articles, may quickly allude to a persuasive purpose. For example, in the *Science News for Kids* article "Cell Phones on the Brain" (Ornes, 2011, April 7), the author states in the first paragraph:

> When cell phones are on, they emit energy in the form of radiation that could be harmful, especially after years of cell phone usage.

Many authors are not as forthright. You will not read statements such as "My purpose is to persuade" or "I think you should believe or do this" or "This is my claim." Instead authors of well-written, complex informational texts are savvy about how they reveal this purpose. They require readers to pay full attention to a text's organization, its details, and even particular words and phrases, to infer their persuasive or argumentative purpose.

Some authors, in the guise of describing or explaining, are also engaged in the purpose of persuading. For example, on the first page of text in *Waste and Recycling* (Hewitt, 2009), the author states the following:

> There is always an important question to ask before throwing something away; can I reduce the waste I make by reusing or recycling it? If you cannot reuse it, then you can save energy and materials and keep the waste out of landfills by recycling it. (p. 6)

Hewitt is making a claim about saving energy and materials and keeping waste out of landfills. Her purpose is to persuade the reader to recycle. In the rest of the book, Hewitt employs an enumerative structure, explaining how young people, the audience for this book, can reuse and recycle particular materials such as paper and cardboard and cellular phones.

In *Angel Island: Gateway to Gold Mountain*, Freedman's (2014) purpose is to describe the Asian immigrant experience after arriving at Angel Island Immigration Station on an island in the San Francisco Bay. Arguably, another of Freedman's purposes is to persuade the reader that Asian immigrants suffered injustices related to racism when they arrived. The author never directly says, "My argument is. . . ." Instead he uses an enumerative text structure that addresses numerous aspects of the immigrants' experience: the paltry living conditions in overcrowded detention barracks, interrogations that lasted for hours, and potentially humiliating physical exams. Freedman reveals his reasoning through the structure of the text and the types of details he has chosen to include.

These texts (and many of the others I have described in this chapter) reveal the need for us to think about the author's purpose as something separate from the text's structure. If we begin by identifying the structure, we may miss an important part of what makes a text complex—the author's purpose. This purpose is external to the text itself and drives the development of both the parts and the whole. Although we may need to read a portion of the text, or preview it methodically, to determine the purpose, reading the text with the purpose in mind advances our understanding in multiple ways.

Recommendations for Instruction

Employ the Language of an Author's Purpose

It is important to use the language of an author's purpose when you introduce a text to a class, a group, or a student. When I give lessons with informational text as the focus, I post the author's purpose for all students to view. For example, in a seventh-grade lesson, before reading aloud a chapter from *Marching for Freedom* (Partridge, 2009), I posted the chart in Figure 3.1, stating the author's purpose. In a second-grade lesson, I posted the chart in Figure 3.2 before reading aloud a

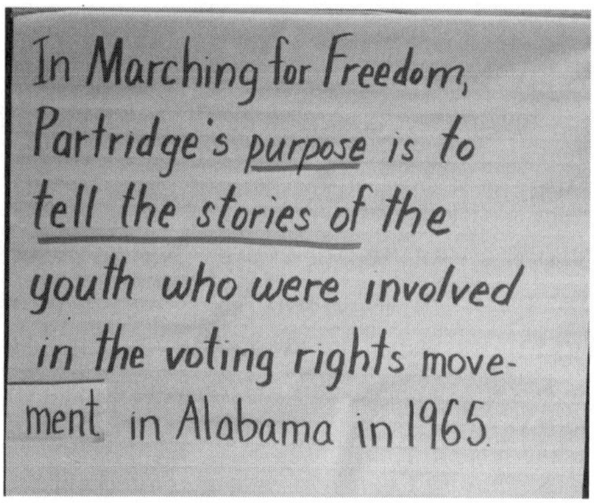

> In *Marching for Freedom*, Partridge's <u>purpose</u> is to <u>tell the stories of the youth who were involved in the</u> voting rights movement in Alabama in 1965.

FIGURE 3.1. Chart stating the author's purpose in *Marching for Freedom*.

> In the book <u>Volcanoes</u> by Peter Murray, the <u>author's purpose</u> is <u>to explain</u> how volcanoes are formed.

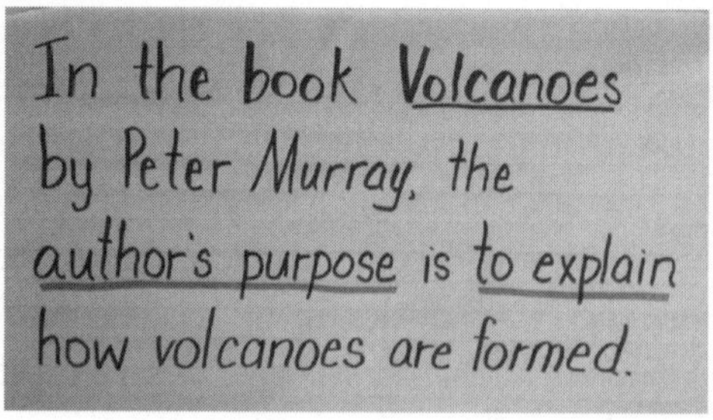

FIGURE 3.2. Chart stating the author's purpose in *Volcanoes*.

passage from *Volcanoes* (Murray, 1996). Restated as questions, these statements can become a purpose for listening to the text read aloud: *What are the stories of the youth involved in the voting right movement in Alabama in 1965? How are volcanoes formed?*

In the classroom, I do not make a big deal about finding a text that fits every purpose or teaching one purpose (over and over) at a time. If you are using a wide variety of texts, most or all of the purposes will surface. Start by making the five genres of purpose part of your language when you introduce texts. Then gradually make this language part of your extended conversation with students by asking questions such as:

"What do you think is the author's purpose in this text?"

"Why do you think so?"

"What in the text makes you think so?"

"Might the author have more than one purpose? Why do you think so? What in the text makes you think so?"

Engage in Shared, Partner, and Independent Writing of the Author's Purpose

Integrate writing about the author's purpose into class lessons. Students might write their thoughts on a sticky note at the end of an interactive read-aloud. They might do so as part of a written response to a text read during reading workshop or during a small-group lesson. During one lesson focused on *purpose*, I worked with a small group of fifth grade students who were reading self-selected texts from *The Scientists in the Field* series. (Figure 3.3 is an outline of the lesson.)

Each student in this group was about a quarter of the way into his or her book when we met for a discussion about author's purpose; having read some of the text already was important because the students had some grasp of the content and could use this to think about the author's purpose. I started by asking them to tell me what they thought the author's purpose was for writing the book—"the reason why the author wanted to write about this topic for a reader." As each student shared, I began jotting down, on a blank piece of paper, the phrases "to explain" or "to persuade" or "to describe" or "to recount." ("To instruct" did not emerge, so I did not write this down.) Figure 3.4 shows the informal notes I made during this conversation.

As each student shared, I restated what the student had said as a question, using the language of purpose. For example, one student was reading *The Dolphins of Shark Bay* (Turner, 2013) and explained that the author's purpose was "to

---

Objectives of Lesson

- Students will identify and explain the author's purpose(s) in a particular text, using language like *to instruct, to recount, to explain, to describe,* and *to persuade.*
- Students will provide textual evidence to support their identification of the author's purpose(s).

Preparation

- Before this lesson, engage students in reading selected informational texts independently. They may all be reading the same text, or they may be reading self-selected texts from a text set.

Procedures

1. Initiate a conversation about the author's purpose.
   - *Why do you think the author wanted to write this text?*
   - *What was the author's purpose in writing this text?*
2. As the conversation proceeds, listen carefully and determine points in the conversation when you can introduce a particular author's purpose. Examples of what this might sound like are:
   - *When you said the author wants to save the dolphins, that made me think he is trying to persuade the reader to . . .*
   - *So the author is telling the story of this journey—he is recounting the experiences of this group.*
   - *The author's main topic is . . . and at this point, the author moves on to a new subtopic . . . so his structure is enumerative.*
3. Take notes during the conversation listing the purposes that surface and jot down students' comments that reveal the purpose. (See Figure 3.4 as an example.)
4. Gradually release by asking students to explain the author's purpose(s) in a written response. (See Figure 3.5.)
5. Regroup. Using the students' notes, discuss the value of this lesson. Close the lesson by asking questions such as:
   - *How did listing and identifying the author's purposes help you talk and write about your book?*
   - *How might thinking about the author's purpose help you understand a different text?*

FIGURE 3.3. Lesson plan: Articulating the author's purpose.

tell readers that these dolphins are rare and amazing and need to be protected." I responded, "So you are saying that the author is trying *to persuade* readers to protect these dolphins?" Her eyes lit up and she nodded emphatically. As we clarified which purpose each student's point would fit under, I jotted notes under that purpose on the paper along with comments (in quotation marks) particular students made. What emerged from this experience was the students' discovery that the authors had more than one purpose.

The students also began to use the language of purpose, both orally and in writing. Before our small-group discussion, the students had already begun a reading response letter. After our discussion, each added a note explaining his or

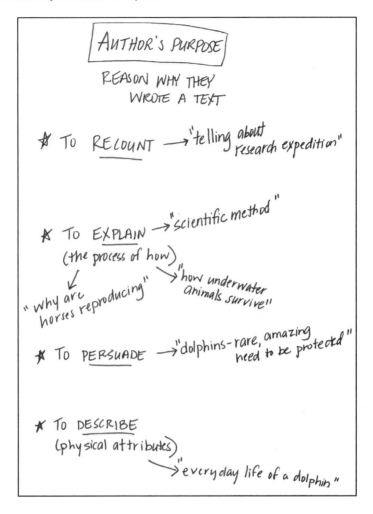

FIGURE 3.4. Notes on an author's purpose during a fifth-grade lesson.

her response to the author's purpose. Figure 3.5 shows two students' attempts. Clearly they are grappling with making this language their own and will need continued opportunities to explore and articulate an author's purpose orally and in writing. At the end of the 15-minute discussion, when I asked the students how using the five categories of author's purpose had helped, one student stated, "It [the five purposes] organizes your thinking so that you can get more out of the writing!"

Create Anchor Charts with Students

I suggest creating an anchor chart with authors' purposes together with your students; the "kid-friendly" language in Table 3.1 might serve as a guide. Specific

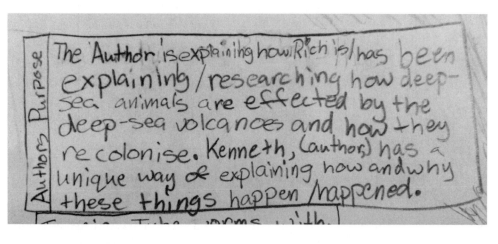

FIGURE 3.5. Two students' responses to the author's purpose.

titles of texts you have read aloud, or that students have read with a partner or independently or in small groups, could be added to the chart over time. You might start shared writing of content for this anchor chart by saying the following:

> "Today we read Peter Murray's text on volcanoes. His purpose was *to explain* how volcanoes are formed. Together, let's define what it means when an author has a purpose *to explain*."

CHAPTER FOUR

What Do We Mean
by a Text's Structure?

A text's structure is the way that a text is organized—how its components are arranged, and how they are interrelated. This structure is determined by the author's purpose. Commonly taught structures include:

- Enumerative.
- Sequence/chronology/narrative.
- Comparison.
- Causal relationships.
- Problem–solution.

The purpose and structure of a text are tightly connected so as to move the reader forward in understanding the content. For example, if the reader knows that the author's purpose for writing *Angel Island* (Freedman, 2014) is to describe the experiences of the people who entered the United States through the immigration center at Angel Island, she will expect to read descriptions of the different aspects of those immigrants' experiences. Even if the reader has only a superficial understanding of Freedman's purpose when she begins the book, this understanding will deepen as she recognizes his structure and begins to expect the author to describe additional experiences.

There are a few complications regarding this theory, though:

- Informational texts for second- through eighth-grade students are frequently not organized into the traditional structures listed.
- Authors of these texts may not use what we call "cue" words or phrases that signal the use of a particular structure or pattern.

- Authors may use an overarching text structure but also employ a different structure for a particular section of the text.
- Authors may employ traditional text structures, such as comparison or causal relationships, at the *micro* or *detail level* (more on this in Chapter Five), but this constitutes only a part and not the whole of the text's structure.

In this chapter I describe each of the traditional text structures (summarized in Table 4.1) and less familiar ideas related to how authors adapt and modify these structures to meet their purpose for writing a text. It is important to note that we need to think about text structures flexibly. Employing our knowledge of text structures adaptively allows us to more easily recognize how a particular text works—that is, what the author is trying to do to achieve his or her purpose and to convey the main ideas in the text.

Enumerative Structure

Enumerative texts provide a general examination of a topic. This type of structure serves primarily as an overarching structure for a whole text, whether book or article length. Typically, the author introduces a topic and then proceeds to discuss the subtopics. According to *Merriam-Webster.com,* the definition of *enumerative* is "naming [things] one after another in a list" (n.d.). If you open to the Contents page of *Rocks and Minerals* (Symes, 2008) and glance at the titles of the first several sections of the book, the subtopics look very "list-like":

Contents

6
The Earth

8
What are rocks and minerals?

10
How are rocks formed

12
Weathering and erosion

14
Rocks on the seashore

16
Igneous rocks

18
Volcanic rocks

TABLE 4.1. "Kid-Friendly" Explanations of Traditional Text Structures

Structure	Explanation
Enumerative	The author uses this structure to teach the reader about a topic or issue. After introducing the topic or issue, the author writes about subtopics or different aspects of the main topic or issue. The content for each subtopic builds on the previous subtopic or content in the text.
	Example: In Seymour Simon's (2000) *Bones: Our Skeletal System,* the topic is the skeletal system. Some of the subtopics are the backbone, the rib cage, and the hand bones.
	In Russell Freedman's (2014) *Angel Island: Gateway to Gold Mountain.* His topic is Asian immigrants' experiences when they arrived at Angel Island, a main entry point for immigrants on the West Coast. His subtopics include a description of the people who came there, the screening process, changes in immigration policy, and the restoration of Angel Island after it sat vacated for decades.
Sequence	With this structure, the author describes a series of steps in a process or episodes related to an event. Authors may use a sequence as a structure for most of their text or just part of their text.
	Example: In *How to Make Bubbles* (Shores, 2011), the author writes step-by-step instructions for how to make bubbles. The whole book is focused on these steps.
Chronology/ narrative	A chronology text structure is also a sequence, but in this structure, the author wants to examine a sequence of events during a specific time period.
	Example: In *Beyond Courage: The Untold Story of Jewish Resistance during the Holocaust* (Rappaport, 2012), the author lists the chronology of the Nazis' rise to power. She writes in a general way as if to inform the reader of a series of events that occurred.
	A narrative is a type of chronology. The difference is a narrative is more story-like, telling the "story of" a group or individual. The author of *Beyond Courage* (Rappaport, 2012) also uses a narrative style to tell the stories of particular Jews who resisted the Nazis, such as Walter Süskind, who, in 1942, figured out a way to smuggle babies out of Amsterdam in the occupied Netherlands.
Comparison	An author employs a comparison structure to examine how two or more objects (or ideas) are the same and different. Many authors use the comparison structure in short parts of their text instead of as a structure for their whole text.
	Example: In *Exploring Glaciers* (Mis, 2009), in just two paragraphs, the author compares two types of glaciers: ice caps and ice sheets.

(continued)

TABLE 4.1. *(continued)*

Structure	Explanation
Causal relationships	An author uses a causal text structure to explain why something occurred. There may be more than one cause and one effect in this structure.
	Example: In *Titanic: Voices from the Disaster* (Hopkinson, 2012), the author reveals how the ice hitting the *Titanic* caused the ship to sink (one cause with one effect), but also that there were many other causes of the deaths of the passengers. These causes included the ship's insufficient number of lifeboats, flooding in the bulkhead compartments, and frigid temperatures.
Problem–solution	When an author uses the problem–solution text structure, he or she identifies a problem and then explains how the problem was solved or could be solved.
	Example: In *Gray Wolves: Return to Yellowstone* (Goldish, 2008), the author describes how removing the wolves from the national park changed the natural environment. Then she explains the steps scientists took to reintroduce wolves to this ecosystem, including holding the wolves, by packs, in acclimation pens and using radio collars to track their whereabouts when they were released.

Suggestion: I recommend replacing the examples of specific texts (as needed) with developmentally appropriate texts for your students, texts you have used during instruction, or texts relevant to your units of study. For this part, you might also consider asking students to write about a particular text's structure and placing it on the anchor chart.

While many enumerative texts have clear subheadings, which identify the subtopics being discussed, others have no subheadings. For example, *Bones: Our Skeletal System* (Simon, 2000) does not use subheadings. If the reader is paying attention and understands the enumerative structure conceptually, she should begin to recognize this pattern in the book. First the author talks about subtopic "A" related to bones, then he moves to subtopic "B," and then subtopic "C," and so forth, working through a list of subtopics related to his primary topic. Although the book does not have subheadings, strong topic sentences indicate the author's subtopics. For example, in the passage included in Chapter One, the topic sentence is:

> Your backbone, or spine, is a flexible column of bones that runs down the middle of your spine. (n.p.)

The text's content on this subtopic (the spine) includes four paragraphs. The next subtopic is identified in this sentence:

> Your rib cage forms a protective shell for some of your most important organs. . . . (n.p.)

Note that each subtopic in an enumerative text not only builds toward a deeper understanding of the main topic, but also frequently builds on the previous sub-topic. In *Bones,* the discussion of the rib cage (immediately after the discussion of the spine) includes the following sentence:

> The rear end of each rib is attached to a vertebra. (n.p.)

If you have read the previous section about the spine, you will recognize the term *vertebra* and maybe even remember that it is "hard and hollow, like a bead or spool of thread" (n.p.). A mental image of the vertebra, one of 33 that make up the spine, will help you construct an even more sophisticated mental image of the rib cage.

Although the two texts just discussed focus on science, a multitude of social studies texts use an enumerative text structure as well, including Scholastic's *You Wouldn't Want to . . .* series. Most textbooks also have an enumerative structure. In all of these texts, the subtopics help to build meaning in some way, advancing the reader's understanding of the main topic.

Sequence, Chronology, and Narrative Structures

In a sequence text structure, an author describes a series of steps in a process or a series of events. For example, *How to Make Bubbles* (Shores, 2011) is a sequence structure presenting a series of steps in the process of making bubbles, whereas *The Great Fire* (Murphy, 2010) is a narrative structure that recounts the events during the 31-hour fire that started on Sunday, October 8, 1871. The authors determine which type of sequence structure to use based on their purpose for writing a text. Frequently, the sequence structure in second- through eighth-grade informational texts is more complex than "first, then, next." Below I explain some of the complexities.

Sequence Structure

In some complex informational texts, the linear flow of a sequence may be interrupted or may be more complicated than a straight sequence structure. In *How to Make Bubbles*, the author employs a linear sequence without any interruptions. By comparison, the sequence in Gail Gibbons's (1993) *From Seed to Plant* is not as linear. The author's purpose is to explain how a seed becomes a plant, and she begins by providing helpful background knowledge. In the first five pages, she describes seeds—their location on the plant, their shapes, and their types—as well as the parts of the plants they become. After this, she begins the sequence structure of the text by describing pollination. In Figure 4.1, I outline part of Gibbons's sequence in order to reveal the complicated nature of her text. Here are a few points to consider while you examine this graphic:

- Notice that after the "pods break open," there are nine possible "next steps." As students read through these steps, they have to retain the initiating step in their minds: the pod breaking open.
- Notice that after students read the nine possible "next steps," the author does not turn to the next step of the seed coat breaking open. Instead she departs from the sequence to describe the parts of a seed and the conditions a seed requires to sprout.

The differences in text structure between *How to Make Bubbles* and *From Seed to Plant* reflect the author's purpose. Shores's purpose is *to instruct* the reader on how to make bubbles. To meet her purpose, she needs a linear sequence of steps for the reader to reach the designated outcome. Gibbons's purpose is *to explain* the complex life cycle of a seed. She needs a sequence structure, but the structure needs to be flexible enough to explain all the possible outcomes that might occur.

Sometimes authors employ a sequence structure at the *micro* or *detail* level; in other words, they embed a short sequence into the larger text. Both *How to Make Bubbles* and *From Seed to Plant* are examples of sequence structures at the macro level, with most of the text organized into this structure. For contrast, consider an excerpt from the book *Things That Float and Things That Don't* (Adler, 2013). The author's purpose is to explain the concept of density—that is, an object's weight relative to its size. In the first six pages of the book, Adler taps the reader's background knowledge (the reader probably knows that "boats full of people float") and Adler also helps the reader acquire new knowledge ("make a list of items in your house that will or will not float when you put them in a sink of water"). Then, building on this knowledge, he introduces the concept of density in the following passage (the word *density* is **bold** in the original text):

> Get a piece of aluminum foil. Form it into a very loose ball. Place it on the surface of the water. It floats.
>
> Now crush the loose ball into a very tight ball. Place it on the surface of the water. It sinks.
>
> The aluminum foil weighs the same whether it's a loose or a tight ball. But the second ball takes up a lot less space. Its **density**—its weight relative to its size—is much greater than the first ball. The density of the second ball is greater than the density of the water. That's why it sank.[1]

---

[1] From *Things That Float and Things That Don't*. Copyright © 2013 by David A. Adler. Used by permission of Holiday House, Inc.

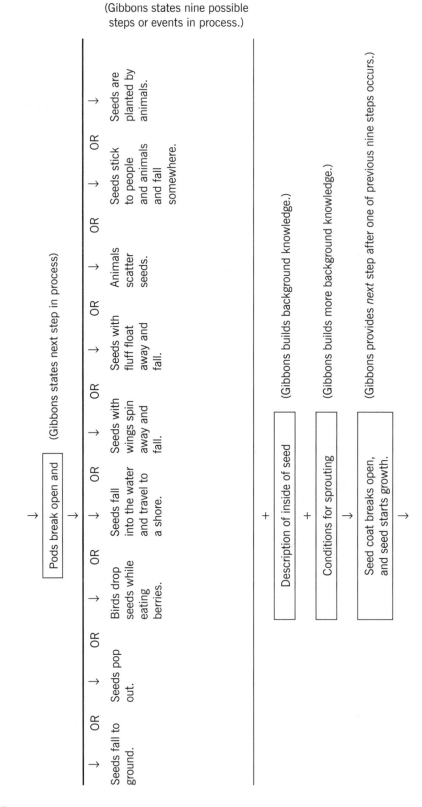

(Gibbons states nine possible steps or events in process.)

(Gibbons states next step in process)

→ OR → OR → OR → Pods break open and → OR → OR → OR → OR → OR →

Seeds fall to ground.

Seeds pop out.

Birds drop seeds while eating berries.

Seeds fall into the water and travel to a shore.

Seeds with wings spin away and fall.

Seeds with fluff float away and fall.

Animals scatter seeds.

Seeds stick to people and animals and fall somewhere.

Seeds are planted by animals.

+

Description of inside of seed   (Gibbons builds background knowledge.)

+

Conditions for sprouting   (Gibbons builds more background knowledge.)

→

Seed coat breaks open, and seed starts growth.   (Gibbons provides *next* step after one of previous nine steps occurs.)

→

FIGURE 4.1. Part of sequence from Gibbons's (1993) *From Seed to Plant*.

50

Notice what Adler has done here. A sequence of steps that might feel familiar to the reader—crushing aluminum foil into a loose or tight ball and testing whether or not it sinks—is used to introduce the concept of density and its role in whether or not an object will float. Adler's sequence of steps was not important for the outcome, but for what it could illustrate. In the rest of the text, Adler explains density by giving examples of things that float and things that don't and then examining each object's density. He purposefully intersperses "do this" sequences into the text to deepen the reader's engagement with, and understanding of, this abstract concept.

Notice the lack of "cue words" in these passages. Traditionally, explicit markers such as *first, second, third* or *first, then, next* have been taught to students as a way to identify a sequence structure. In the excerpt from *Things That Float and Things That Don't* (Adler, 2013), the author uses only one marker: *now*. This lack of markers or cue words contributes to the complexity of texts. Readers have to recognize the imperative tone—the command or request to follow steps ("Put some water in a paper cup"). Even in a much simpler text such as *How to Make Bubbles* (Shores, 2011), the author only uses the word *next* once.

Chronology and Narrative Structures

When an author uses the chronological text structure, he or she arranges and describes events in the order of their occurrence. In many history texts, particularly textbooks, chronologies are list-like; the text reads something like "first this happened on this date, and next this happened on this date, and then this happened on this date." General terms are often used to identify the agents involved (e.g., "the Germans" or "the troops" in a text about World War II), and a distant, formal register makes these events seem as though viewed from afar.

A narrative is a *type* of chronological structure in that it usually follows a timeline of events. However, a narrative provides a closer-up view, telling the personal stories of the agents involved. The narrative structure tends to include the elements of plot we attribute to fiction, with historical figures as the characters or agents and actual events that serve as the inciting forces, the rising actions, and the climactic moments. The use of a narrative structure is, of course, closely aligned to the author's purpose, but recounting events as a purpose and using narrative as a structure are still distinct.

In *Beyond Courage: The Untold Story of Jewish Resistance during the Holocaust*, Doreen Rappaport (2012) employs both chronological and narrative structures. Her primary purpose in this book is to tell the stories of Jews who resisted the Nazi regime. The following passage comes from a narrative about one man, Walter Süskind, who, in 1942, devised a way to smuggle babies out of Amsterdam in the occupied Netherlands:

Süskind learned the schedule of the streetcars that stopped in front of the day-care center. At the precise moment that a tram blocked the view of the guards in front of the theater, a messenger would leave the day-care center with a "bundle" and hop on a streetcar. It was easiest to smuggle out babies and small children. They were often given a drop of wine to make them drowsy and then hidden in suitcases, backpacks, laundry baskets, or sacks of potatoes. (p. 25)[2]

The narratives in this book span the time period from 1933 to 1943 and are divided into groups: stories of Jews who realized that Hitler was a threat, stories of Jews who lived under German occupation, stories of Jews placed in ghettos, and stories of Jews sent to death camps. Important to note is how Rappaport contextualizes the groups of narratives by inserting short chronologies of what was happening at that point in the larger world. For example, there is a section of *narratives* called "Part Two: Saving the Future" with stories from occupied Netherlands, Belgium, France, and Poland. (The passage about Walter Süskind is from this section.) At the beginning of this section, though, prior to the narratives, is a two-page *chronology* titled "Hitler's Campaign for World Domination" (pp. 18–19). I have excerpted the following phrases or sentences from each paragraph in this chronology. Notice the difference between the previous excerpt about Süskind and the ones below; I have put specific words and phrases in **bold** for this purpose.

- "**Simultaneous** with his methodical degradation of Jewish life, Hitler shaped his campaign for world domination. Defying the Treaty of Versailles, he rebuilt Germany's armed forces and, **in 1936**, sent thirty thousand troops to take back the Rhineland, one of Germany's former territories, from France" (p. 18, paragraph one).
- "**On March 13, 1938**, Germany incorporated Austria as part of the Nazi plan to . . ." (p. 18, paragraph two).
- "**Six months later, in March 1939**, Hitler broke his promise. . . ." (p. 19, paragraph two).
- "**In August 1939**, Germany and the Soviet Union signed a nonaggression treaty renouncing war against each other" (p. 19, paragraph three).
- "But Hitler was not satisfied. **In 1940**, he invaded and conquered Denmark, Norway, France, Holland, Belgium, and Luxembourg" (p. 19, paragraph four).
- "**In June 1941**, Hitler betrayed his pact with the Soviets and attacked the Soviet Union. **By 1942**, most of Europe was held or led by Germany or pro-Nazi regimes" (p. 19, paragraph four).

---

[2] Excerpt from *Beyond Courage: The Untold Story of Jewish Resistance During the Holocaust*. Copyright © 2012 by Doreen Rappaport. Used by permission of Candlewick Press.

As in a typical chronology, Rappaport clearly marks time order, and she refers to the agents and groups of people with broader (but still distinct) terms, such as "thirty thousand troops." Her clear timeline of events develops the idea that Hitler was making progress in his "campaign for world domination." (Within 4 years, he was in control of most of Europe.) Rappaport's tight use of dates, along with other details and choices of language at the micro or sentence level, helps to reveal the clear speed with which Hitler's regime came into power. Noticing this, a reader can begin to grasp the gravity of the situation for the Jewish resistance and empathize more clearly with people such as Süskind.

Rappaport's use of both narrative and chronology structures meets her purpose. While recounting the personal stories of those who suffered under the Nazis, her employment of the chronologies serves to contextualize the people, places, and events described in the narratives. The intentional composite structure of chronologies and narratives creates a cohesion that allows the reader to put everything together and begin to think critically about the main ideas in the text.

Some authors use the narrative structure as a frame for describing or explaining a science or social studies concept. There are a slew of books and articles that narrate the endeavors of particular scientists, engineers, and historians. Consider this passage from the *National Geographic Explorer* article "Extreme Ice" (Geiger, 2013):

> Michele Koppes's kayak moves next to a glacier. A chunk of ice falls. It hits the water near her. Koppes keeps paddling. She studies glaciers. She knows how dangerous glaciers can be.
> Glaciers are huge rivers of ice. They are made from layers of snow. The layers press together. Over time, the snow turns into thick ice. (p. 18)

Notice how the author begins with a narrative about Michele Koppes who, with a team, is studying how glaciers move and change, but then briefly introduces the reader to the concept of glaciers. Later she returns to the story about Koppes. The author continues to use this back-and-forth process throughout the article. Geiger actually blends two structures: enumerative and narrative. In each section of the text, while she narrates the research team's experiences hiking and climbing across a glacier, she also includes descriptions of particular aspects of the glaciers—their physical attributes, how fast they move, and the effects of their movement on the landscape.

Comparison Structure

In a comparison text structure, an author describes the similarities and/ or dissimilarities between two or more objects or ideas, examining various

qualities of those objects or ideas. In complex texts, comparisons are more often embedded as details in a text rather than as overarching structures. In other words, not many texts focus primarily on comparing objects or ideas. Typically, the use of comparison serves a purpose that supports the author's larger purpose for the text.

Authors may want to explain the physical or conceptual differences between two objects or ideas. In *Exploring Glaciers* (Mis, 2009), the author's purpose is to describe glaciers, and the text's macro or overarching structure is enumerative. Threaded throughout the text are micro-level comparisons of different types of glaciers, as in the following passage:

> Ice sheets are huge, flat glaciers that cover large pieces of land. They are the biggest glaciers on Earth. There are only two ice sheets in the world. They are in Greenland and Antarctica. The Antarctic ice sheet covers around 5.4 million square miles (14 million sq km). It is more than 2 miles (3 km) deep in some places!
>
> Some people mix ice caps up with ice sheets. Ice caps cover large areas, too, but they are smaller than ice sheets. An ice cap is shaped like a dome or plate, and ice caps are considered to be mountain glaciers. (p. 8)[3]

This comparison, even at the micro level, is complex. Notice that the author describes "ice sheets" in the first paragraph and then cues the reader in the second paragraph that she is going to address a difference: "Some people mix ice caps up with ice sheets." She then states a difference explicitly with the clause "but they are smaller than ice sheets." But in the last sentence, in order to understand the difference in shape between an ice sheet and an ice cap, which is "shaped like a dome or plate," the reader must *look back* to the first paragraph and note that ice sheets are "flat." In order to infer why an ice cap might be considered a "mountain glacier" (and how that is different from an ice sheet), the reader also has to *look ahead* to the next section of the text (not quoted here), which focuses on mountain glaciers.

Some authors may use a comparison to support a larger theme or idea in a text. As noted earlier, Freedman's purpose in *Angel Island: Gateway to Gold Mountain* (2014) is to describe Asian immigrants' experiences when they arrived at the immigration station and also to persuade readers that these immigrants were treated unjustly. Although this is an enumerative text, Freedman employs comparisons in short parts of the text. In the passage below, he contrasts Angel Island with Ellis Island. Notice how his use of this comparison serves his purpose:

---

[3] Excerpt from *Exploring Glaciers* by Melody S. Mis. Copyright © 2009 by The Rosen Publishing Group, Inc. Used by permission.

Angel Island was often called the Ellis Island of the West, but the two immigration stations were very different. Immigrants who passed through Ellis Island in New York Harbor came mainly from Europe. They were usually processed in a few hours or, at most, a few days, and then they boarded a ferry to Manhattan and set out for their new lives.

Immigrants arriving at Angel Island came mainly from China and other parts of Asia. It was the job of inspectors at Angel Island to enforce the strict Chinese exclusion laws, along with other laws passed later that limited immigration from all Asian countries. As a result, Angel Island served as a detention center, where newly arrived immigrants might be held for weeks or months while they tried to prove their legal right to enter the country. "Would it be possible," a Filipino immigrant asked, "for an immigrant like me to become part of the American dream?" (p. 20)[4]

Freedman contrasts the two immigration stations to reinforce his purpose; as a result, a main idea can emerge for the reader. Freedman does not use explicit markers to identify the comparison structure, but, as in the passage from *Exploring Glaciers*, he requires the reader to infer the differences between the stations by looking back and forth at the information in each paragraph.

Sometimes an author uses a comparison not to explain the difference between two actual objects or ideas being compared, but because it aids our understanding of a larger concept. In *Things That Float and Things That Don't* (Adler, 2013), the author's focus is on teaching the reader about the concept of density. He contrasts the density of different objects, such as marbles and pails, to make his point about how density—the relative weight of an object to its size—affects whether an object will float or not. The point is not to learn that marbles will sink and pails will float, but rather *why* one floats and the other sinks.

Causal Relationships

An author uses a causal text structure to explain why something occurred. In complex informational texts for intermediate and middle grade texts, very rarely do a single cause and a single effect make up a text's structure. Instead most of these texts are structured with multiple causes and effects, as well as the various factors that may have contributed to the causes. For this reason, I use the term *causal relationships* instead of cause–effect. Students need to understand that a text's structure may not be as simple as (one) cause–(one) effect.

---

[4] Excerpt from *Angel Island: Gateway to Gold Mountain*. Copyright © 2014 by Russell Freedman. Used by permission of Houghton Mifflin Harcourt Publishing Company. All rights reserved.

Sometimes one cause has several effects that lead to a larger effect. In *The Wolves Are Back* (George, 2008), the author's purpose is to explain the effects of removing wolves from the wilderness in national parks. When the numbers of wolves in and near national parks were decimated, the ecosystem changed drastically. With no wolves as predators, the elk herds grew and overgrazed on the grasses. With no grasses to eat and use for nests, the Vesper sparrow disappeared. With no wolves as predators, the buffalo trampled young aspen trees so more grass would grow. Without aspen trees, the flycatchers disappeared. Without the grass and trees, erosion occurred along the riverbanks. And so forth. Readers have to understand that the initial or root cause was the removal of the wolves from a delicate ecosystem and the ultimate effect was a different environment. In between there was a causal chain of incidents.

Sometimes there are multiple causes for a final effect. For example, in *Titanic: Voices from the Disaster* (Hopkinson, 2012), the author explains that hitting the iceberg (cause) led to the ship's sinking (effect), but there were many causes for the deaths of the crew, staff, and passengers. These causes included insufficient lifeboats on the ship, flooding in the bulkhead compartments, and frigid temperatures. The text also describes the "what-if" factors. What if the operators in the radio room had not been too swamped with passenger messages, and had paid closer attention to a message from another ship warning of large icebergs nearby? What if the crew of *The Californian,* a ship just 10–20 miles from the *Titanic,* had recognized the eight distress signals sent by its neighbor instead of assuming they were "some sort of company private signals" (p. 101)?

Frequently, causes and effects are not signaled but are implied, requiring the reader to draw conclusions. Consider this excerpt from George's (2008) *The Wolves Are Back.* Just before this passage, the author tells the reader that the Vesper sparrow has returned to Lamar Valley after a 100-year absence. Then she continues by explaining the reason for the absence and the return in the following:

> The vast elk herds had eaten the grasses the little bird needed for food and nesting materials. When the wolves returned, they frightened the elk up into the mountains. The grasses grew tall. The sparrow raised babies and sang. (n.p.)

The second sentence clearly states a cause and effect with a causal connective "when" (when the wolves returned, then the elk left). In the first and third sentences, though, the reader has to infer the effects of the elk eating the grasses (the little bird disappeared) and the effects of the grasses growing taller (the sparrow returned to the valley).

Even at the macro level, as in Hopkinson's (2012) *Titanic*, most of the causal relationships are implied. Because of the length of the narrative (book length) and the many factors involved, it would be redundant for Hopkinson to be explicit about cause and effect. Instead she lets the reader infer the many effects of the ship's sinking, the poor preparation for disaster, missed opportunities, and so forth.

Problem–Solution Structure

When a problem–solution text structure is employed, the author identifies a problem and then explains how the problem was or might be solved. Inherent to this structure is the presence of causal relationships. A problem is an effect. Many times identifying what caused the problem aids in developing and enacting a solution. For example, in *The Wolves Are Back*, the absence of the wolves in the environment was a problem, caused by the national park directors' decision to get rid of the wolves. The effect was a significant change in the environment. The solution was to reintroduce wolves to the national parks, which caused the return of animals that had disappeared.

It is important to consider what we mean by the word *solution*. According to *Merriam-Webster.com* (n.d.), the word *problem* is defined as "something that is difficult to deal with." The word *solution*, as it relates to a problem, has two definitions. One is "an answer to a problem" and the second is "the act or process of solving a problem." Whether an author highlights the solution as "an answer" or as "the *process* of solving" depends on his or her purpose for writing the text.

For example, in *The Wolves Are Back*, the author's purpose is to explain the effects of removing and then returning the wolves to the national parks. In one sentence, she briefly mentions the "answer" that solved the problem: "In 1995, ten adult wolves were brought down from Canada and set free in Yellowstone National Park" (n.p.). So while she states the *answer* to the problem—returning the wolves to Yellowstone—she does not explain the *process* of solving this problem because that is not her purpose.

By contrast, in *Gray Wolves: Return to Yellowstone* (Goldish, 2008), the author's purpose is to explain "the process of solving" the problem of a changed ecosystem due to lack of wolves in Yellowstone Park. After giving some background information on why the wolves were removed and the problems that resulted, Goldish details the steps scientists took to reintroduce wolves to this ecosystem. The process of solving the problem included holding the wolf packs in acclimation pens and using radio collars to track their whereabouts when they were released.

Problems and solutions are inherent to texts with narrative structures. While telling the story of Prohibition in *Bootleg* (2011), Blumenthal explains the many factors that led to the passage of the Eighteenth Amendment. Members of the Women's Christian Temperance Union and the Anti-Saloon League believed that consumption of alcohol was detrimental to the health of the community (the problem). The ultimate goal of these groups (and the perceived solution to the problem) was to add an amendment to the Constitution prohibiting the sale of alcohol. As we know, they succeeded and the amendment became law in January 1920. The purpose of Blumenthal's text is not the simple identification of a problem and a "solution as answer," though. Her purpose is to create a vivid picture of *how* these groups achieved Prohibition. A multifaceted process was involved. Groups and individuals engaged in agitation, ransacking saloons, and spoke and rallied in public, like many other activists before them. They also learned to fundraise to support their efforts and to lobby for legislation and enforcement of this legislation. They found power in the vote and campaigned for "dry" candidates. In the end, this persistent drive toward their goal led to the ratification of this amendment.

The term *solution* does not necessarily connote *resolution* (or a clear-cut, happy ending to a problem). In *Bootleg*, Blumenthal describes how, initially, statistics showed a drop in arrests related to drunken behavior and a decrease in the amount of alcohol consumed. But then this changed, as individuals and groups began to act subversively to gain access to, and to sell, alcohol. Prohibition caused a whole range of new problems (effects). Some of these problems were solved by the repeal of the Eighteenth Amendment; other problems persist into modern times, leading to the development of groups such as Mothers Against Drunk Driving (MADD).

In *The Case of the Vanishing Golden Frog: A Scientific Mystery* (Markle, 2012), the problem is that these frogs are dying from a microscopic fungus. The solution is to house the frogs in a facility, nursing those that are sick back to health, and then keep them there permanently because of their susceptibility to this fungus in their natural environment. The solution is a temporary one—and a problem in itself with no foreseeable permanent solution.

Recommendations for Instruction

Think Flexibly about Text Structure

Trying to find a one-to-one fit between a text and a structure can lead to a sense of futility. Instead, students should think about text structures *conceptually* as well as *flexibly*. How is an author organizing his or her ideas at the macro level to support his or her purpose and to convey main ideas? How is the author integrating particular structures at the micro level to strengthen his or her overall structure? Keep in mind that enumerative, sequence/chronology/narrative, and problem–solution structures are the most frequent structures at the whole-text level. Comparison and causal relationships are more frequently found at the micro or detail level. And then there are texts that do not seem to fit any structure. I work with students to discover (or notice) how an author has structured a text. Sometimes the students and I end up naming one of the traditional structures and that helps us progress in understanding the text as well as other texts. Sometimes naming a traditional structure is not as helpful, and we create our own structure instead, based on our analysis of the text. Our understanding of traditional structures has generative value and helps us to do this. I describe in detail shortly two lessons I experienced with a group of fifth-grade students; Figure 4.2 outlines a similar lesson plan.

Rename and Redefine the Term *Text Structure*

The graphic organizers that we typically use to teach text structure have a static presence. For example, there might be a box for the problem and a box for the solution. I think our vision of structure needs to be more fluid as we think about each *particular* text's structure. In our language with students, as we discuss a wide variety of texts, perhaps we should even shift from the terminology *text structure* to *a text's structure*. A text's structure evolves as we continue to read, developing gradually from a simple to a more complex form. Sometimes the language we use regarding structure and the graphics we present for particular structures constrict this thinking. Students begin to think about fitting square pegs into round holes. We might want to consider changing how we define *a text's structure* as well, as the following possible definitions suggest:

- A text's structure is the organization of the text's parts, along with how they are interrelated.
- A text's structure is the way in which the text is built by the author—its components, and how they are arranged and are interrelated.

My purpose in crafting these definitions is to highlight the interrelatedness of the parts or components that make up a text. I want to make clear that texts vary in structure and that whereas the *parts* of a text may present new information in themselves, they also contribute to the construction of larger ideas.

Objectives of Lesson

- Students will explain how a particular text is structured.
- Students will gain a deeper understanding of the content of a text because they can articulate how it is structured to serve the author's purpose and convey main ideas.

Preparation

- Locate an appropriate text.
- Be prepared to lead a discussion about how the text is structured, using the language of structure. Study the text. I recommend creating your own graphic organizer and using it to take notes about how the author structured the text.

Procedures

During the first lesson, coach students in strategically reading and learning the content of the text.

During the second lesson:

1. Initiate a conversation about the text's structure with prompts such as:
   - *What did you notice about the structure of the text?*
   - *How did the author organize the information in the text?*
   - *How did the author develop the ideas in the text?*
2. As the conversation proceeds, model your own thinking about the structure with language such as the following:
   - *I noticed the author started by . . .*
   - *I noticed how the author moved forward by . . .*
   - *I noticed how the author closed by . . .*
   - *Here the author used a . . . (comparison, causal relationships, problem–solution) detail . . .*
   - *At this point, the author moves on to a new subtopic by . . .*
3. Model taking notes about the text's structure for students. If appropriate, decide on how to represent the text's structure with a hand-drawn graphic organizer (see Figures 4.3 and 4.5). Encourage students to take similar notes.
4. Gradually release by asking partners to take notes about particular sections of the text. Clearly review their purpose for reading closely and taking notes.
   - *Remember to think about the structure the author is using to teach you the content. How is the author organizing the parts or ideas in the text? How are these parts or ideas related?*
5. Regroup. Using the students' notes, discuss the overarching organization of the text. Close the lesson by asking the following questions, to which students can respond orally or in writing:
   - *How did thinking about the text's structure help you understand the content better?*
   - *How might the experience of analyzing a text's structure help you read other texts?*

FIGURE 4.2. Two-day lesson plan: Analyzing a text's structure.

Use Conversation to Help Students Notice a Text's Structure

Before I began a small group lesson with fifth graders, I had the students independently read the article "Active Earth" (Geiger, 2010) in an issue of *National Geographic Explorer Magazine, Pathfinder Edition*. The author's purpose in this article is to explain why the Earth is active. A main idea (at the gist level) is that the Earth is always moving because the tectonic plates are affected by the molten rock in the core and mantle. Geiger employs an *enumerative text structure* that introduces the topic of the active Earth and then addresses subtopics related to this concept. Each section clearly adds new content to that in the previous section.

Before assigning the students to read the article independently, I shared the author's *purpose* for the article. After they read the article, I started our meeting by asking the students to tell me what they learned from the text related to the author's purpose. When they started talking animatedly, sharing specific details and noting main ideas, I quickly realized that they understood Geiger's content. Yet when I asked them to tell me how the author structured her text to develop these ideas, they were clearly unsure.

I next proceeded to engage the students in a conversation about the text's structure, but I did not name or define the enumerative structure yet. Instead, we talked about how one section built on the next. As we talked, I jotted down notes on a piece of paper; the students wrote notes, too. I asked questions such as "What is this section mostly about?" and "How did the last section help us understand this section?" Through conversation, the students began to realize that the author starts out large, explaining how the Earth was formed over millions of years; then zeroes in close, introducing, naming, and comparing the Earth's layers to a boiled egg; and then zooms in closer, explaining how the movement of the crust is affected by the molten rock in the mantle and core (cause). Then the author describes the slow movement of the plates, but how, over time, this movement accumulates. In summary, she identifies the main topic early in the article and then addresses subtopics, linking each to the previous one. I asked the students to summarize what we had discovered so far about the author's development of the main idea. As they did, I noticed they were using the same words I had to explain Geiger's structure, such as *introduce, explain,* and *compares.* I jotted these words down on a sticky note like the following:

cause	effect
introduces	examples
defines	because
	explains

When I asked the students if these words helped them articulate the author's idea development, there was a resounding "yes!"

My point here is that taking the time to have conversations about how a text is structured and integrating into that conversation the language with which authors construct and organize their texts is invaluable. In addition, adding shared writing of notes or jotting down this language as you talk with students is another way of supporting their growing ability to articulate a text's structure—orally and, as you'll see next, in writing.

Use Writing to Help Students Articulate a Text's Structure

Writing about a text's structure and content requires students to step back and organize their thinking and then rearticulate their thoughts even more clearly than they may have done orally. During the lesson I just described, I split the fifth-grade students into two small groups to explore and explain the development of ideas in the last four sections of the article "Active Earth." Each group took a sticky note on which I had jotted the key words we had used during our conversation. When the groups returned their sticky notes to me later, I noticed that they had added more words to help them articulate their thinking; they used the notes as a tool and by adding words to the tool, adapted its use to their purposes.

When we regrouped, the students were able to explain to me how the author continued developing the main idea in the second part of the article. Figure 4.3 shows one student's notes regarding the development of content over the course of the article. He describes the content in each section; I asked him to add the arrows to create a sense of flow, or a sense of development. The student finished by writing about the author's development of the text at the top of his paper (next to the asterisk). Figure 4.4 shows another student's synopsis of the how the author has structured the text. Here she has employed the language I used—"zooms in"—during our conversation to articulate her thinking. She is appropriating the language from our conversations and over time should require less support in doing this.

Provide Opportunities to Discover Structure While Learning Content

On the next day, during a second lesson with the fifth-grade group of students, I introduced and explained the term *enumerative text structure*. Then the students and I engaged in a conversation about what made the article "Active Earth" an example of enumerative structure. They quickly understood how the term applied to the article because they had teased out the structure for themselves during the prior lesson. Before the second lesson, the group had read "The Winning Edge"

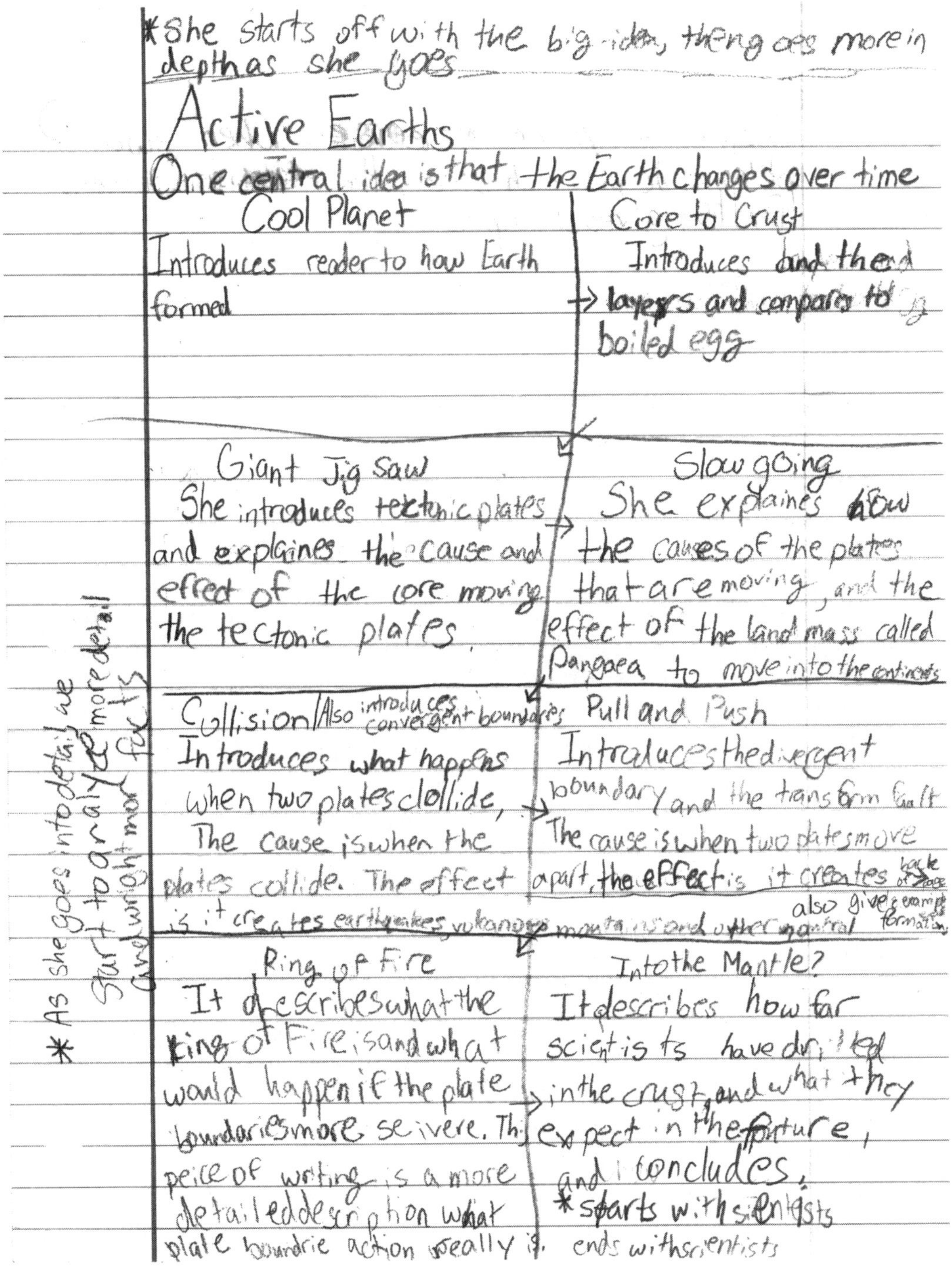

* She starts off with the big idea, then goes more in depth as she goes

Active Earths

One central idea is that the Earth changes over time

Cool Planet	Core to Crust
Introduces reader to how Earth formed	Introduces and the → layers and compares to boiled egg
Giant Jig saw She introduces tectonic plates and explaines the cause and effect of the core moving the tectonic plates.	**Slow going** She explaines how the causes of the plates that are moving, and the effect of the land mass called Pangaea to move into the continents
Collision /Also introduces convergent boundaries Introduces what happens when two plates collide. The cause is when the plates collide. The effect is it creates earthquakes volcanoes mountains and other general	**Pull and Push** Introduces the divergent boundary and the transform fault The cause is when two plates move apart, the effect is it creates back of page also gives example formation
Ring of Fire It describes what the Ring of Fire is and what would happen if the plate boundaries more seivere. This peice of writing is a more detailed description what plate boundrie action really is.	**Into the Mantle?** It describes how far scientists have drilled in the crust, and what they expect in the future, and concludes. * starts with scientists ends with scientists

As she goes into detail we start to a rais more detail and we right more facts

FIGURE 4.3. One student's notes on the development of content in the article "Active Earth."

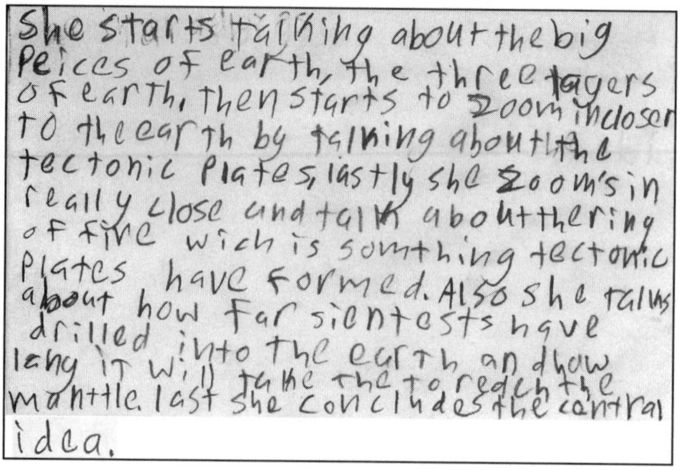

She starts talking about the big Peices of earth, the three layers of earth, then starts to zoom in closer to the earth by talking about the tectonic plates, lastly she zoom's in really close and talk about the ring of fire wich is somthing tectonic plates have formed. Also she talks about how far sientests have drilled into the earth and how long it will take them to reach the mantle. last she concludes the central idea.

FIGURE 4.4. One student's synopsis of the author's text structure in the article "Active Earth."

(Gilbert, 2010), another article in the same issue of this magazine. Now that I had introduced the term *enumerative text structure,* I challenged the students to examine the new article's structure and evaluate whether or not the author had employed this structure.

The author's purpose in the article "The Winning Edge" (Gilbert, 2010) is to explain Newton's laws of physics as they apply to one athlete's experience training to compete in an event that includes ski jumping and cross-country skiing. The text's structure is enumerative, with each section addressing aspects of the skier's training and/or one of Newton's laws of physics. The content about the athlete made this text's structure difficult to identify because students felt as though they were reading a "story about" this person. In discussions with one another, though, the students realized that the story of (i.e., narrative about) this athlete's training was a frame for learning about Newton's laws. By reading to see how the author organized or built the text, they discovered that each section of the article really dealt with a different subtopic of the overarching topic.

I asked the students to get into their small groups (from the first lesson) again and create a graphic with details that illustrated the structure of this text. Figure 4.5 shows two students working on a graphic they created. The overarching topic is in the center, and there are spokes to circles containing the subtopics. I asked them to add arrows to reinforce the point that the subtopics provide more information not just about the overarching topic, but also about each other.

My purpose in both of these lessons was not to teach a particular text structure, but to facilitate a deeper understanding of the author's content and main ideas *through an understanding of the text's structure.* I worry that sometimes when

FIGURE 4.5. Students work on a graphic to illustrate text structure.

we introduce structures, our students start looking to fill in the blanks. There seems to be more power in letting students discover structures and their value initially, and then using this knowledge as a lens for thinking about what they are learning as they read additional texts.

This discovery can happen during discussions about rigorous texts that have been read aloud and during guided reading or small-group conversations. The ultimate goal is for students to have access to the language they need to describe the structure of the text they are reading, as a way to deepen their understanding of the author's purpose, content, and main ideas.

CHAPTER FIVE

What Types of Details Are in Non-Narrative Texts?

In complex informational texts authors include different types of details to create meaning for the reader at the micro or sentence level. The author's purpose continues to drive the development of the text even at this level. Let's consider another text by Seymour Simon (2005), *Guts: Our Digestive System*. The author's purpose is to describe the many parts of the digestive system, such as the teeth, salivary glands, and esophagus, and to explain how digestion works. As with *Bones: Our Skeletal System* (Simon, 2000), this text has an enumerative structure and, again, the author employs a variety of details at the micro level. As you read the following sentence from *Guts*, notice the details Simon has employed:

> The pointed canine teeth just beside the incisors are good for ripping and tearing at food. (n.p.)

What *types* of details does Simon include just in this one sentence?

- Name of a part of a system—*canine teeth*.
- Physical attribute of the part—*pointed*.
- Location of the part—*just beside the incisors* (the term "incisors" was explained in the sentence immediately before this one excerpted above).
- Purpose of the part—*ripping and tearing at food*.

This sentence contains a lot of information. To unpack sentences with multiple clauses, readers will find it helpful to keep in mind the author's purpose—in this case, to describe and explain the digestive system—as well as the types of details the author uses to serve that purpose. So a reader might summarize what he or she has learned from this sentence by saying:

> "I know that the author is trying to describe the different *parts* of the digestive system to me, and here he is clearly describing a specific tooth: the canine. He creates a picture of these teeth by sharing their *shape* (pointed) and their *location* (beside the incisors, which I just read about). He also tells me the *function* of these teeth (tearing food), which I infer is helpful in digestion."

Words such as *parts, shape, location,* and *function* provide the language for readers to categorize the content they are learning and to articulate what they are learning.

It is difficult to categorize these details according to a particular topic, genre, or structure, as they overlap the categories abundantly. In this book, I examine *types of details* in two groups: those in non-narrative texts and those in narrative texts. Figure 5.1 lists general types of details in (but not limited to) non-narrative texts.

The details in this list and the one in Chapter Six (on narrative texts) are not exhaustive. Instead, they are intended to provide language for the reader to use to describe what she is learning about a topic or the content of the text. These

---

- Name of topic
- Name of subtopic
- Location
- Function, purpose, or behavior
- Duration, or when something takes place
- Physical attributes (movement or action, color, size, shape, number, texture, composition, etc.)
- Construction or organization
- Explanation of how something works (may include causal relationships, sequence of details, and variables)
- Real-life examples
- Comparisons (including similes and metaphors)
- Other types of figurative language (alliteration, onomatopoeia, and personification)
- Quotes from experts (for the purpose of sharing relevant knowledge or just sharing an opinion)
- Attempts by author to connect with reader

FIGURE 5.1. General types of details in (but not limited to) non-narrative texts.

lists will expand as readers think through complex texts, noticing and naming the types of details authors use to convey content and main ideas.

Details in Texts about Systems

Some texts are written to describe a system, a set of parts that form a whole, such as the skeletal system, the circulatory system, or the parts of a plant or cell. To meet this purpose, an author might include details about the following:

- Name of the system or a part of the system
- Location of the system or parts of the system
- Physical attributes of the system or parts of the system (color, size, shape, number, texture, composition, etc.)
- Function of the system or parts of the system

Simon's *Bones* (2000) and *Guts* (2005) are good examples, as are his other texts *The Brain: Our Nervous System* (2006a) and *The Heart: Our Circulatory System* (2006b). Another example already mentioned is Gibbons's *From Seed to Plant* (1991). In a detailed illustration, she describes the *parts* of a flower, their *locations* (with labels and words such as "at the top"), and their *functions*. Descriptions such as these are plentiful in science textbooks and other texts for middle grade students. In *Genetic Engineering* (Cohen, 2010), part of the *Let's Relate to Genetics* series, the author describes the different parts of a cell, including chromosomes (the word *proteins* is in **bold** in the original text):

> Chromosomes are tiny beaded threads made of **proteins**. Chromosomes carry the cell's genetic material, known as DNA. A typical human cell has 23 pairs of chromosomes—a total of 46. (p. 10)

In these three sentences, Cohen does the following:

- Names the part of the cell—"chromosomes."
- Physically describes the part—the chromosome.
  - Size—"tiny."
  - Shape—"beaded thread."
  - Composition—"made of proteins."
  - Number—"a typical human cell has 23 pairs of chromosomes."
- States the function of chromosomes—"carry the cell's genetic material, known as DNA."

To summarize, a reader using the language of types of details to articulate her thinking might say the following:

> In this paragraph I learned about *parts* of the cell called the chromosomes. The chromosomes are small in *size* and *shaped* like a thin line of beads threaded together. They are *composed* of proteins, and there are usually 23 pairs in every human cell.

Details in Texts about Mechanisms

In texts that describe a mechanism—a system of parts that work together as in a machine—the author's purpose is to describe the mechanism and explain how it works. Some types of details the reader might notice include:

- Name of the mechanism
- Names of its parts
- Its function
- Its construction
- How it works (which may include causal relationships or sequence details)

In the following passage from Macaulay's (2013) *Toilet: How It Works*, notice the details he uses to describe the toilet and explain how it works.

> Most toilets have two containers of water. The one on top with the handle or button is called the tank. The part you sit on is called the bowl. Do not sit on the tank!
> Once you have finished, you flush.
> The tank holds almost two gallons of water. When you push the handle down, a chain inside the tank pulls up a stopper. *Whoosh!* All the water rushes into the bowl and all the waste disappears. Pretty impressive, don't you think? (pp. 9–10)[1]

What details has Macaulay included in this excerpt?

- Name of the mechanism—"toilet."
- Name of its parts—"tank," "bowl," "handle," "chain," "stopper."
- Its construction—"two containers of water": "one on top" and "the part you sit on," the "handle" that pushes and is connected (implied) to the "chain inside," which is connected (implied) to a "stopper."

[1] Excerpt from *Toilet: How It Works*. Copyright © 2013 by David Macaulay. Used by permission of Roaring Brook Press. All rights reserved.

- How it works—"When you push the handle down, a chain inside the tank pulls up a stopper."
- Its function (implied)—"all the waste disappears."

What about the final sentence in the passage: "Pretty impressive, don't you think?"? I might have a discussion with students about how to "name" this type of detail, in which an author is trying to engage the reader in a conversation. We might use the following:

- Connecting with the reader.

Identifying this type of detail and adding it to a list of details we have noticed and named reminds the reader that she is involved in a learning experience with the author, who is aware of her presence.

Details in Texts about Processes or Transformations

In these texts the author's main purpose is to explain a type of transformation. For example, in *From Seed to Plant*, Gibbons (1991) moves from describing a system (a flower and its parts) to explaining the transformation of the seed to a plant through pollination, and so forth. Some of the details readers might notice include:

- Name of process
- When it takes place and its duration
- Location
- Explanation of the actual process or transformation (which may include causal relationship details or a sequence of events)
- Function
- Results
- Real-life examples

In the *National Geographic Explorer* article "Active Earth" (Geiger, 2010), the author's purpose is to explain how the actions of the Earth's tectonic plates result in changes in the landscape. Geiger employs an enumerative structure in discussing different type of boundaries where the plates meet: convergent boundaries, divergent boundaries, and transform fault boundaries. Notice the types of details she has included in each phrase or sentence (the words *convergent boundary* are **bold** in the original text):

A **convergent boundary** is where two plates collide. A collision between two continents is a real head-banger. It causes the plates to push upward.

That's what's been happening as India crunches into the Asian plate. The plate carrying Asia has been pushed up. Way up. In fact, the collision has created the towering Himalaya mountains! (p. 12)

What types of details did the author employ?

- Location of process—"convergent boundary."
- Description of process (this is also a "when" and a "cause" detail)—"where two plates collide."
- Result (effect)—"plates push upward," "towering Himalaya mountains."
- Real-life example of this transformation—"as India crunches into the Asian plate," "plate carrying Asia has been pushed up," "has created the Himalaya mountains."

How would a reader name the detail in the second sentence: "A collision between two continents is a real head-banger"? This is a comparison in the form of a simile. I would encourage students to add this as a type of detail and watch for it when thinking carefully about a text:

- Comparison (simile)—"A collision between two plates is a real head-banger."

Details in Other Non-Narrative Texts

There is an endless array of texts that do not fit in the three categories: systems, mechanisms, and processes. We could also list categories of details for texts describing animals or habitats. For example, what types of details do you notice in the following passage about the weevil? What would you name these details?

A weevil is a herbivore. It has a long snout that curves downward. Some weevils have a snout that is longer than their body. (Bix, 2013, p. 6)

There could be another set of details describing people, places, and cultures. What do you notice in the passage below about the ruins of Tenochtitlan, the Aztec empire? What would you name these details?

Buried beneath what is now Mexico City, below the corridors and tunnels of the subway system, lie the ruins of the greatest city of the Aztec empire—Tenochtitlan (ten-och-tee-TLAN). (Sands, 2002, p. 2)

The point is to encourage students to ask "What type of information is the author providing?" and "How is this information contributing to the larger topic or idea the author is discussing?" Another critical thinking point for students is to ask, "What patterns of detail use am I seeing in multiple texts on the same topic?" There are no right answers for naming a type of detail or a category of details— except that the name has to make sense and move the reader forward in understanding. Figure 5.2 provides a compilation of the categorized types of details. You can use these as a lens for thinking about the details authors use in texts in your classroom.

Details in Texts about Systems

The author's purpose is to describe a system or parts of a system, such as the digestive system, a cell, or a plant.

- Name
- Location
- Physical attributes (color, size, shape, number, texture, composition, etc.)
- Function

Details in Texts about Mechanisms

The author's purpose is to describe a mechanism—a system of parts that work together in a machine—and to explain how this mechanism works. Examples of mechanisms are septic systems, clocks, and bicycles.

- Name of the mechanism
- Names of its parts
- Function
- Construction
- How it works (may include causal relationships or sequence of details)

Details in Texts about Processes or Transformations

The author's purpose is to explain a process. Although these texts can be a blend of genres, there is a major focus on some type of transformation, such as how a seed becomes a plant, how volcanoes are formed, or how a bill becomes a law.

- Name of the process
- When it takes place and its duration
- Location
- Description (may include causal relationships or sequence of events)
- Function
- Results
- Real-life example

FIGURE 5.2. Some types of details in (but not limited to) non-narrative texts about systems, mechanisms, and processes. These details are based on the work of Anderson and Armbruster (1984).

Recommendations for Instruction

During Planning, Study and Name Types of Details for Yourself

Because students *need* language to name what they are noticing, I study the texts I will be using with students, annotating for the types of details and making sure I have language to offer them during instruction. Figure 5.3 shows my notes from a fifth-grade lesson.

When the teacher and I met before I planned the lesson, we discussed assessment data and her personal observations about the students as readers. There was a trend: Many were struggling to recall details in their science texts. At that point in the year, the students were engaged in a unit of study on cells. When I read the text the teacher was planning to use and thought about what would make it complex for these students, I realized how dense it was with details about animal cells. Yet the types of details were clear. There were details about the *parts* of a cell, the *location* of the parts, and the *function* of the parts. When I read an additional excerpt about plant cells the teacher planned to use in a follow-up lesson, I noticed overlap with the types of details used in the first text. To facilitate my own study of the text and to guide my teaching during the lesson, I annotated the text and wrote notes.

In each of the lessons described in the rest of this chapter, I had my own notes by my side to help me guide students forward. Notes are an invaluable tool—both the final product that I can reference while teaching as well as the learning I go through as I develop the notes. I come away from planning with a deeper insight into the text and what might make it complex for students.

Engage Students in Reading Closely, Annotating, and Sketching in Response

During a series of three lessons with second graders studying land forms, we engaged in close reading of complex sentences to identify types of details, as in this excerpt we unpacked from *Volcanoes* (Murray, 1996):

> Sixty miles beneath our feet lies a layer of hot, half-molten rock called the mantle. Enormous crustal plates, thousands of miles across, float like rafts on this ocean of soft stone, fitting together like the pieces of a giant jigsaw puzzle. (p. 9)

Figure 5.4 is a list of the details we generated together, which expanded each day. I asked the students to sketch what they had learned from the excerpt. This turned out to be a teachable moment as some of the students began drawing what they already knew about volcanoes versus what we had learned from the text excerpt. I stopped the class and talked about sketching details from the text

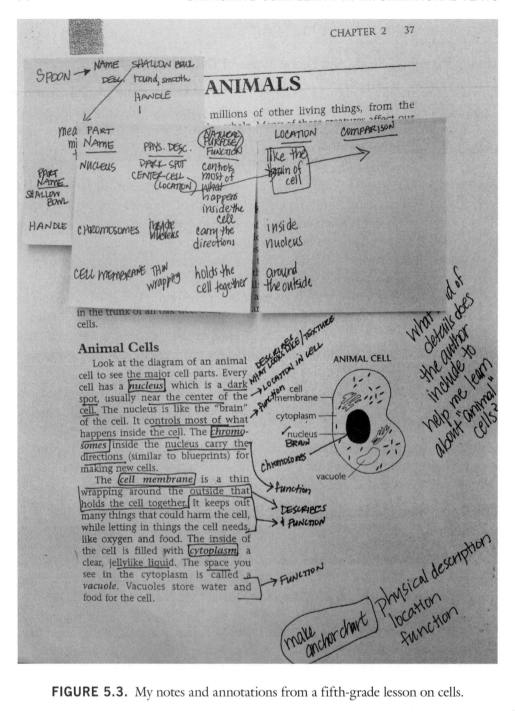

FIGURE 5.3. My notes and annotations from a fifth-grade lesson on cells.

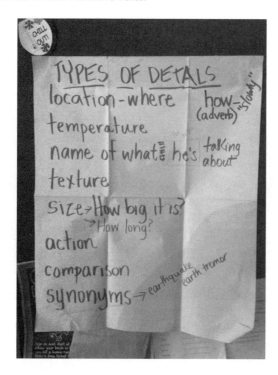

FIGURE 5.4. List of details generated in a second-grade class with an excerpt from the text *Volcanoes* (Murray, 1996).

using evidence in the text to support their sketches. There was a notable shift in their thinking from that moment forward.

To reinforce this point, at the beginning of the next two lessons I asked three students to place their annotated excerpts and sketches on the document camera and share with their peers how they used the details in the text to help them identify what to draw (see Figure 5.5). With continued coaching, the students grasped this concept. In Figure 5.6 (from the third lesson), notice how the sketches and labels are connected to the text.

On the second and third days, the students also had an opportunity to read a book from a text set on volcanoes and other land forms with a partner. As I conferred with the students, I asked, "What types of details are you noticing?" This question was difficult for many students, especially because the texts were by different authors with a variety of purposes—not just the purpose of explaining how volcanoes are formed. For example, some texts included stories about volcanoes erupting. Still, the students had an awareness of the need to unpack complex sentences. Over time, with coaching and guidance during small-group lessons, students became more independent in slowing down and thinking through the details an author is including. The students in this class persevered during these

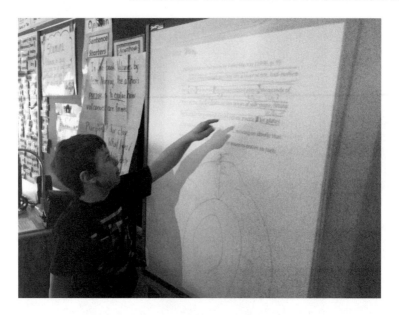

FIGURE 5.5. A student showing his peers his annotations and sketches on the document camera.

lessons, and I had a moment of joy when one girl approached me with her book and said, "I found some details!"

It is noteworthy that during these lessons we went from experiencing the *whole* text excerpt to the *parts* of the text excerpt and then returned to the *whole* text excerpt. We engaged in shared and partner reading of the passage before moving into close reading. We talked about the larger ideas in the passage before reading phrase-by-phrase and annotating. Then we returned to the larger ideas in the text when we sketched the "whole" with the "parts." Figure 5.7 is a suggested plan for a similar 3-day cycle of lessons.

"Transfer" Learning to Other Topics or Theme-Related Texts

With another second-grade group, I taught a similar series of lessons with texts focused on animals. Similar to the 3-day lesson cycle described in Figure 5.7, the routine for each lesson looked like the following:

- Reading aloud a few pages from the anchor text *Snakes* (Bishop, 2012).
- Close reading of a short excerpt about an animal (with the excerpt projected on the document camera and a copy for each student).
- Shared writing of a list of types of details (as we annotated during close reading).

FIGURE 5.6. A student's annotated excerpt from *Volcanoes* (Murray, 1996).

- Sketching and labeling (with teacher present to coach).
- Reading from leveled texts about animals with a partner.

The excerpt we chose for the first lesson was three sentences from Bishop's text. See Figure 5.8 for one student's interpretation of the size of scales on the belly of the snake versus those on the rest of the snake. A teachable moment surfaced multiple times in all three lessons when students did not recognize details that tell "where"—for example, words such as *in* were difficult for the students. As a result, we began to annotate our list of details, adding examples of words that indicated particular types of details. (We did this during the lessons with the other second-grade class as well.)

To promote students' sense of agency, for the second lesson we chose an excerpt from a (generally considered) second-grade-leveled text, *Aye-Aye*

Objectives of Lesson
- Students will recall details from a complex sentence.

Preparation
- *Develop a class set of texts on the same topic.* These texts should be at various reading levels and will be used by students to read with a partner at the end of each day's lesson.
- *Choose one text as an "anchor text."* This is a text you will read aloud at the beginning of each lesson and a text from which you may choose an excerpt for close reading. There is no need to finish reading the entire text during this cycle of lessons.
- *Select two excerpts from the anchor text or from a text in the text set.* You will be modeling and gradually releasing responsibility to partners on Days One and Two. These texts can be a tad more rigorous than the excerpt for Day Three because of the amount of support students will be receiving.
- *Select excerpts for partners to close read* on Day Three. For my lesson, the reading specialist located a leveled text for the each of the guided reading groups the teacher already met with regularly. In the leveled book room, she found quite a few texts on animals. Then she copied one page from each leveled text for partners to read closely.

Procedures

Day One (Whole Class and Partners)
- Interactively read aloud several pages from the anchor text.
- Lead the whole class or a small group in close reading of the text excerpt (from the anchor text or from a text on a similar topic).
- During close reading, begin a chart listing the types of details noticed and named.
- Coach students as they sketch in response to the excerpt read closely.
- Confer with partners or individuals as they read texts selected from the set.

Day Two (Whole Class and Partners)
- Interactively read aloud several pages from the anchor text.
- Lead the whole class or a small group in close reading of the text excerpt (from the anchor text or from a text on a similar topic). Release some of the responsibility to partners by asking them to read and annotate the last part of the excerpt on their own. Continue adding to the chart with the list of types of details.
- Coach students as they sketch in response to the excerpt read closely.
- Confer with partners or individuals as they read texts selected from the set.

Day Three (Whole Class and Partners)
- Read aloud from anchor text.
- Ask three students to share their annotated excerpts from the previous lesson. Prompt them to share how their sketch is supported by the text.
- Review the details listed on the chart during the previous two lessons.
- Coach partners as they close read an excerpt from an appropriate level text.
- If possible, pull a small group of students together to work with closely while the other students work with their partners.

FIGURE 5.7. Three-day lesson cycle: Identifying types of details in complex sentences.

Excerpt #1 *Snakes* (Bishop, 2012, p. 10)

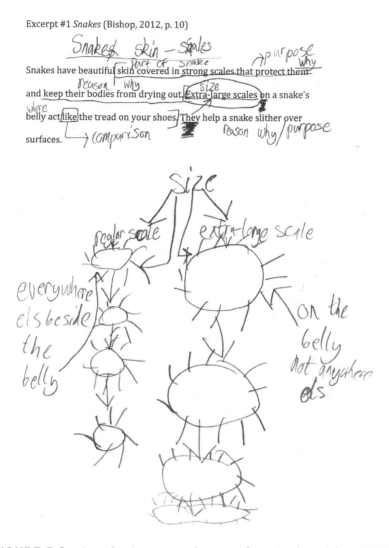

FIGURE 5.8. A student's annotated excerpt from *Snakes* (Bishop, 2012).

(Robinson, 2013) and incorporated a gradual release of responsibility. After leading a close reading of the first section of the text with students, I assigned them to work individually or with partners to annotate the second section. I also gathered a small group to meet on the carpet. Figure 5.9 is one student's annotated, sketched, and labeled excerpt. She colored the eyes yellow and made it clear to her readers that the aye-aye (a type of lemur native to Madagascar) is awake and that it is nighttime in her picture.

For the third lesson, we copied short excerpts from multiple-leveled texts—depending on the instructional level of each pair of students. The reading specialist came in and met with one group while I met with another group. We also had the luxury of having a classroom teacher who could confer with pairs. The point is that groups and pairs could meet if teachers and specialists partner in the classroom.

This approach to teaching is applicable in second through eighth grades. With the previously mentioned lesson for the fifth-grade class studying cells, I created categories of words that describe the part of a spoon called the "bowl" as an analogy for the types of details authors employ in writing about cells. In about 3 minutes, the students and I described the physical attributes, location, and function of the bowl of a spoon, and I wrote these details on a chart (see Figure 5.10). We then applied thinking about "types of details an author uses to teach" to a short text on animal cells. The teacher followed up with a similar lesson using a short text on plant cells. With the second text, the students quickly realized the overlap in types of details. There was a sense of achievement, and the teacher noted that one result was a stronger recall of the facts in the text.

FIGURE 5.9. A student's annotated excerpt and drawings for *Aye-Aye* (Robinson, 2013).

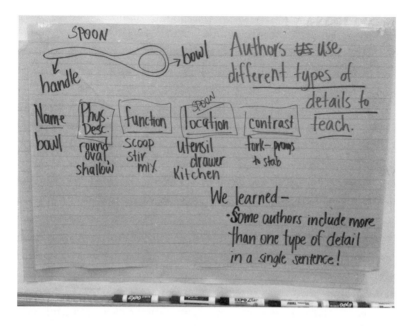

FIGURE 5.10. "Types of details" chart using the parts of a spoon.

At the beginning of a three-lesson cycle with a group of seventh-grade students, I facilitated close reading of the Science News for Students article "Cell Phones on the Brain" (Ornes, 2011). (This article can be viewed at *https://student. societyforscience.org/article/cell-phones-brain*.) Ornes's purpose, as we have already noted, is to persuade readers that cell phones might be harmful to our brains when we talk holding them next to our heads. Initially, I asked the students to read the whole article. They easily recognized the author's purpose and central idea. However, when I asked them to talk with me about how the author developed this idea, they were not as articulate. Like many articles on this site, Ornes makes a claim, describes a research study, explains additional information the reader might need to understand the study that supports his claim, and then restates his claim. Of course, there are more types of details interspersed between those I just listed, and this is the tricky part for students. They have to navigate, categorize, designate importance, and so forth. Having the language to name what the author is doing, to name the author's craft, helps in this endeavor.

We engaged in a close reading of the article with the following purpose in mind: If the author's central idea is that cell phones may be harmful, how does he *develop* this idea? Over two lessons (45 minutes each), we noticed and named the types of details the author employed to develop this idea and how the details supported one another. As noted earlier, in all of the lessons I have described, sometimes, when the students are stumped, I have to provide a "name" for what the author is doing. In this lesson, the students realized that the author was quoting an expert who had led a research study on this issue, but they did not have the words *expert quote* in their vocabulary to name what they had noticed. Similarly, at the end of the article, the author lists *alternative options* to listening with cell phones held next to your head. Again, I provided the language once they had noticed this type of detail.

For this particular text, some annotations about types of details were appropriate for sentences or phrases and others were more appropriate for a paragraph. We made these distinctions as we "made sense of the text" together during close reading. Figure 5.11 is a section of one student's annotated text. At the end of each lesson, I asked a student volunteer to come forward with her annotated excerpt. Together, we modeled for the class how to use our annotations (my notes were projected on the document camera) to have a conversation about how the author developed his idea that cell phones might be harmful. These kinds of conversations *improve* students' use of language and ability to articulate what an author is doing to develop an idea—in a particular text and then, hopefully, in texts other than that one.

Again, as we "named" the author's craft during close reading—that is, the types of details he was using—we generated a list on the dry erase board (see Figure 5.12). This list turned out to be a useful reference for the students as I gradually released responsibility for reading and annotating to partners and then individuals. On the third day, I presented the students with a second article from the *Chicago Tribune*, titled "Cell Phone Radiation Could Pose Dangers to Kids" (Deardoff, 2011). (This article can be viewed at *www.chicagotribune.com*; just search the title.) Written in the same time period, just after the study described in the previous article was published, this author has a similar purpose. Many of the students, empowered with the language we had generated to name what an author is doing to develop an idea, quickly took the lead on annotating. As with any group of diverse learners, others needed coaching and would have benefited from continued guidance in a small group. This 3-day cycle of lessons about articulating the author's development of an idea and integrating close reading of two texts on the same topic is outlined in Figure 5.13.

Revisit Particular Types of Details at Students' Points of Need

A teachable moment arose in my conferences with the students who were annotating the second article from the *Chicago Tribune*. A key difference between the two articles is that the second author only briefly describes the research study and also cites more sources. When I asked individuals which author's argument was more credible, they leaned toward the second author because "she quotes more experts." I knew from studying both articles that the second author's "experts" were not as credible. Consider this excerpt from the first article, the Science News for Students article by Ornes, in which he cites an expert:

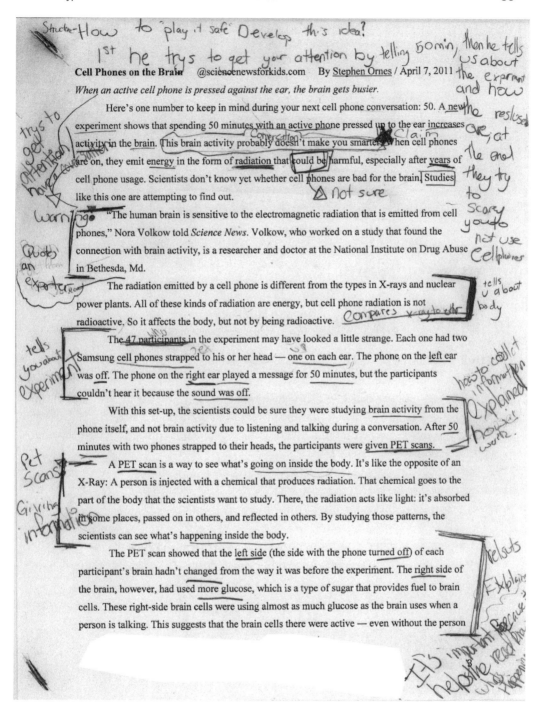

FIGURE 5.11. A student's annotated text from "Cell Phones on the Brain" (Ornes, 2011).

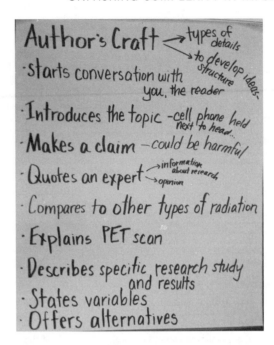

FIGURE 5.12. List of types of details from the seventh-grade lesson on cell phones.

"The human brain is sensitive to the electromagnetic radiation that is emitted from cell phones," Nora Volkow told *Science News*. Volkow, who worked on a study that found the connection with brain activity, is a researcher and doctor at the National Institute on Drug Abuse in Bethesda, MD.

If we analyze these two sentences for the types of details the author uses to develop credibility, these are the points that might surface:

- Quotes researcher discussing an actual study on the topic.
- Provides details about the researcher quoted.
- Establishes Dr. Volkow's expertise as "researcher and doctor."
- Names (what appears to be) a credible institute that employs Dr. Volkow: "National Institute on Drug Abuse."
- Names location of the institute: "Bethesda, Md."

Each of these details supports the credibility of Dr. Volkow and what she has to say about the topic. These details contribute to the credibility of the author's argument. The students and I unpacked these details, and I took notes on the dry erase board. Then we turned to the sources cited in the second article and unpacked those. (Figure 5.14 shows the notes I jotted on the board as the students and I analyzed each author's expert quotes.)

Objectives of Lesson
- Students will articulate, orally and in writing, how an author developed a central idea or argument.
- Students will contrast two texts on the same topic.

Preparation
- *Locate a well-written article* with a clear claim and supporting evidence.
- *Locate a second article on the same topic.* (Once I find the first article, then I search for a second article on a related research study or topic; it does not have to be as well written as the first.)
- *Study both articles* and be able to articulate the types of details the author uses to develop his or her ideas.

Procedures
Day One
1. *Introduce the topic and the article.* (I used a news clip about the research study on cell phones to elicit the students' interest before introducing the article.)
2. *Pose the purpose for the first read.* What is the author's central idea or claim? Why do you think so? Engage the students in a discussion about the author's purpose. Together compose a statement on chart paper that all students can view.

Day Two
1. *Review the lesson from Day One.*
2. *Pose the purpose for the second read.* How does the author develop this central idea or claim? What types of details does he or she use? (It is always helpful to write the purpose for close reading on a board for all students to view and even to ask them to write this purpose at the top of their copy of the article.)
3. *Model reading, thinking, and annotating with a copy of the article on the document camera or smart board for all students to view.* Focus on the purpose for close reading—how the author develops the central idea through the use of particular details.
4. *Construct a class list of types of details the author is using for all students to view* as you model and engage them in thinking aloud with you. (See Figure 5.12.)
5. *Gradually release responsibility.* Assign a few sentences or a paragraph at a time to partners to read and identify the type of detail the author is using to support the claim.
6. *Regroup.*
7. *Model with one student how to use your notes to talk about the author's development of the central idea.* Assign partners to do the same.
8. *Close with independent writing,* by asking each student to write 2 or 3 sentences about the author's development of the claim on a sticky note; students should attach the sticky note to their annotated article.

Day Three
1. *Review the types of details* that were listed during the previous lesson.
2. *Present a second article on the same topic.*
3. *Pose purpose for the first read.* What is the author's central idea or claim? Why do you think so?
4. *Engage the students in a discussion about the author's purpose.* Together compose a statement on chart paper that all students can view.
5. *Purpose for second read with a partner.* How does the author develop this central idea/claim? What types of details does he or she use?
6. *Listen* in to a few discussions; *coach* at the point of need.
7. Regroup.
8. Purpose for small-group discussion: How do the two articles differ in content and idea development? (Depending on the group, you may need to model with a student how to start this conversation using the student's and your notes.)
9. *Listen* in to a few of the discussions; *coach* at the point of need.
10. *Close with small-group conversations.* Assign two sets of partners to meet with each other and discuss their findings.

FIGURE 5.13. Three-day lesson outline: An author's development of a central idea or argument in two texts on the same topic.

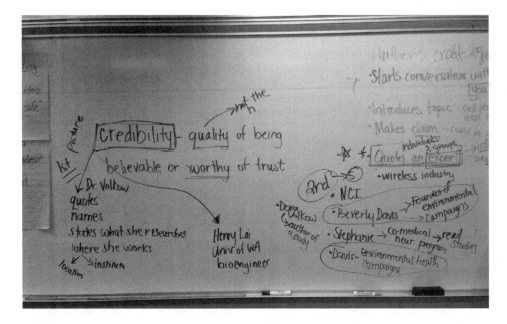

FIGURE 5.14. Notes from a seventh-grade discussion on the credibility of an expert quote.

What we noticed was that although the second author (Deardoff, 2011) had more sources, close examination of the details the author used to describe these sources revealed that they were less credible in supporting her argument. She does cite Dr. Volkow, but she does not give background information to support the researcher's credibility. Another source she cites is not a researcher, but a person who works for an advocacy firm focused on reducing cell phone use by children. She does cite sources with an alternative view to her own, but these sources are vague. And then consider the following sentence:

> The wireless industry group says no research has proven cell phones to be dangerous.

Who is the "wireless industry group"? What is Deardoff's source for this statement? Because we teased out and named the types of details Ornes used (in just those two sentences), many of the students quickly realized the difference in the types of details between the two articles and how those details influence the credibility of an author's argument.

What Types of Details Are in Narrative Texts?

In this chapter, we consider details in narrative texts, focusing primarily on texts about historical events. Although readers may notice an overlap in the types of details in non-narrative and narrative texts, there are still some differences between them. As mentioned earlier in the book, a narrative text typically follows a chronological structure and tells the personal stories of the people or *agents of the events* it describes. In this way, narrative texts tend to resemble the plots we see in fiction.

Frequently Used Details

To start assembling a list of the types of details used in narrative informational texts, let's look again at Partridge's (2009) *Marching for Freedom: Walk Together, Children, and Don't You Grow Weary*. We know that the author's purpose is to recount, or tell the story of, the experiences of youth as they marched for voting rights in Selma, Alabama, in the mid-1960s. The author employs a narrative text structure to serve this purpose. In the book's second chapter, Partridge introduces an adolescent, Charles Mauldin, who had begun to attend Freedom Fighter meetings—a part of the movement to secure voting rights for African Americans. The first obstacle Charles faces in getting involved in the movement is his own disposition toward equal rights. In the following passage, he realizes that he himself has not questioned Jim Crow:

> Charles Mauldin, a quiet, serious student at the all-black Hudson High in Selma, was intrigued. "I always had an answer for everything and I was really stunned because I had no answer for those questions." There were so many aspects of segregation he had blindly followed. Why did he have to step off the sidewalk when a white person walked by? (p. 10)[1]

What has the author done here to develop the idea that Charles is examining his disposition? She:

- Names the agent—"Charles Mauldin."
- Describes his character—"quiet, serious."
- Places the agent in a context—"student at the all-black Hudson High in Selma."
- Describes his disposition in the context of the movement—"intrigued."
- Uses a quote to elaborate on the agent's disposition—"'I had always. . . .'"
- Describes the agent's mindset, or stream of consciousness, as he questions his disposition—"There were so many. . . . Why did he have to . . . ?"

In the next paragraph Charles Mauldin remembers an incident with the Ku Klux Klan; a close reader might identify this type of detail as *an anecdote to support the author's point about Charles's mindset.* Then the depiction of Charles' shifts, as the author reveals in phrases and sentences such as the following (p. 10):

- "At first Charles was intimidated. . . ."
- "Charles and other students were eager to accept the challenge. . . ."
- "Charles spread the word."

Additional details are given about Charles's actions and his effect on other students, who elected him as leader of the Dallas County Youth League. Based on the initial passage I quoted, here is how a student might summarize the author's development of the idea that Charles had to face *himself* as an obstacle and change his mindset:

> "I learned that one of the youth involved was Charles Mauldin, who went to the all-black high school in Selma. The author introduced him to me by describing the type of person he was, his character—quiet and thoughtful— and his disposition toward the movement—intrigued or curious. The author really wanted me to understand Charles's mindset, so she included a quote

---

from Charles that explains how he had never really questioned Jim Crow, and, for Charles, this was a shocking experience to think that things might be different."

If a student can articulate what the author is doing or how the text is constructed in this passage, what happens when the author, just after writing about Charles Mauldin, introduces another adolescent?

> Bobby Simmons, another student at Hudson High, was skeptical that they could change their relationship with whites. "From a child up at that time you was taught to fear them," he said. "Our parents explained to us kids that the white was almost the Great God or the Great Father. If they say we couldn't go places, we couldn't go." (pp. 10–11)

In this case, the student might immediately notice that Partridge is identifying another agent in this context (Bobby Simmons), describing his disposition (skeptical), and using Bobby' statements to explain his disposition. Later in the text there is a shift in Bobby's disposition, too; he is described as feeling that the movement was "exhilarating and empowering" (p. 12).

Why do I use the term *agent*? According to *Merriam-Webster.com*, the definition of *agent* is "one that acts or exerts power" or "one who acts on behalf of another" (n.d.). In texts about historical events, these are frequently the figures we study, and read and think about critically. By identifying Charles and Bobby as *agents*, we are highlighting their role in the situation being described in the text. A discussion of the meaning of *agent* can lead to a discussion of the term *agency*—a historical figure's sense that he or she can change circumstances and achieve a goal.

The terms used to name types of details should be developmentally appropriate. Depending on the sophistication of the students, I might use a simpler descriptor such as *major person involved* or the main person in place of *agent* (in the lower grades). For older students, I would increase the rigor and use phrases such as *describes the agent's character* and *describes the agent's disposition*. In this context, *character* is the type of person one is, whereas *disposition* is a mindset toward a particular issue or in a particular situation. Regardless of the age of the students, I avoid using the term *character* as a synonym for a historical figure or agent; to do so might confuse students who are unclear about the difference between fiction and nonfiction.

Another type of detail that might be integrated into discussions of an author's craft (and content) is *explains agent's motive*. This detail is sometimes packed into lengthy, complex sentences. By unpacking a sentence for the particular details an author uses, readers can uncover the motive. In *Bootleg: Murder, Moonshine, and the Lawless Years of Prohibition*, Blumenthal (2011) writes the following:

In 1893, Howard H. Russell, a Congregationalist minister, founded the Anti-Saloon League in Oberlin, Ohio, with a mission to save people from "the evils of the drink habit and . . . the debauching curse of the drink traffic." (p. 43)

In just this one sentence, Blumenthal has included the following details:

- Names when and where—"1893," "Oberlin, Ohio."
- Identifies agent—"Howard H. Russell, a Congregationalist minister."
- Names agent's action—"founded the Anti-Saloon League."
- Names agent's motive for action—"with a mission to save people from. . . ."
- Uses a quote from agent (as confirmed in source notes, p. 140) to explain the motive—"the evils of the drink habit and . . . the debauching curse of the drink traffic."

Other frequently used details I have noticed and named in narrative texts include the following:

- Introduces another agent in this context.
- Provides an anecdote (short story) to elaborate on a point.
- Includes one or more examples.
- Gives a definition to clarify.
- Departs from the narrative to provide background information.
- Uses figurative language to compare or to enhance understanding in some way.

Keep in mind that there are no hard and fast rules about what to "name" the types of details an author includes. The purpose is to make sense of the content in a text and, as a result, progress toward understanding the author's main ideas.

Details That Reveal an Author's Bias

There are also types of details (language) that reveal an author's bias or viewpoint. For example, any time an author writes about *how* a historical figure felt, the author is interpreting evidence (primary and secondary sources) he or she has gathered and analyzed. Think back to this sentence in the passage about Charles Mauldin in *Marching for Freedom* (Partridge, 2009):

Charles Mauldin, a quiet, serious student at the all-black Hudson High in Selma, was intrigued. (p. 10)

Details that describe Mauldin's character ("quiet" and "serious") as well as his disposition ("intrigued") are Partridge's interpretations of the sources she analyzed for this book. Such language can be considered "loaded" in that it is subjective and packed with possible connotations. By contrast, details that name the agent (Charles Mauldin) and place him in a particular context, such as "the all-black Hudson High," are factual, meaning they are verifiable if we consult reputable sources.

An author's use of generalized versus specific vocabulary can be an important detail to consider when evaluating an author's bias as well. For example, in Rappaport's (2012) *Beyond Courage: The Untold Story of Jewish Resistance During the Holocaust*, she does not use generalized terms such as "the Germans" when she describes Hitler's campaign for world domination. Instead, she refers specifically to "Hitler" and "German forces." When she does refer to the agent "Germany" as taking some type of action, it is after she has already established that she is writing about the agents "Hitler" and the "Nazis." As a result, her reference to "Germany" as an agent does not connote "all people in Germany agreed to do this and took action." Instead, there is a clear sense that here, "Germany" is being used to represent Hitler and his pro-Nazi supporters.

The types of details that are *missing* from a text are another possible indication of an author's bias or point of view. Consider the text *If You Lived at the Time of the American Revolution* (Moore, 1997) from the *If You . . .* series published by Scholastic. In a two-page spread with the subtitle "What did colonial people look like? How they dressed," the illustrations show two families, both with four typical members as well as an additional infant and/or toddler. The different parts of clothes are also labeled. If we survey all the details mentioned in the spread, we notice that only a homogenized group is described, using words such as "most people," "well-to-do people," "boys," "men," "girls," and "women." Although the author does use the qualifier "most"—acknowledging that she is not describing all people—she has still made the choice to include only certain details. What if you were an indentured servant or an African slave living in the time of the American Revolution? What would your clothes look like? Analyzing texts for missing details also presents opportunities for critical thinking.

The types of details found in informational narratives (both factual and interpretive) are not limited to narratives about historical events, of course. For example, in *The Elephant Scientist* (O'Connell & Jackson, 2011), discussed earlier, the authors include many of the details described in this chapter, in their narrative about the team's research expedition in Etosha National Park. At the same time, the authors use many types of details described in the previous chapter for *non-narrative* texts to describe the physical attributes of the elephants and explain how they communicate.

One of our purposes during instruction should be to help students *slow down*—so many of them rush through texts. We need to help students unpack lengthy sentences with multiple clauses and longer texts dense in detail. The power of thinking through and naming details is in the language we use and that our students appropriate as a result. This language—the words we use to name what the author is doing—does not have to be exact. Instead our language should be useful to students in making sense of what the author is doing, facilitating a deeper understanding of the content of a text and the author's main ideas. Figure 6.1 provides suggested language you can use to describe the details mentioned in this chapter. Again, this list is not exhaustive but is intended as a way to launch your own thinking about texts. Here are additional recommendations with anecdotes from my own teaching experiences.

Recommendations for Instruction

Project the Text Excerpts and Model How You Annotate a Text

When you are reading an excerpt closely with students, it is important to project the text using a document camera or smart board (or even an old overhead) for all students to view. In addition, students need to observe you reading a

---

The author . . .

- Names an agent (or a group); introduces another agent.
- Places the agent in a context (when and where; additional details may be included).
- Describes the agent's character.
- Describes the agent's disposition in a particular context.
- Names the agent's action.
- Explains the agent's motivation for action (which usually includes causal relationships).
- Provides an anecdote (with the purpose of elaboration or support or building knowledge).
- Uses a quote (with a purpose).
- Describes the agent's mindset, stream of consciousness.
- Provides a flashback (with a purpose).
- Includes one or more examples.
- Gives a definition to clarify.
- Departs from the narrative to provide background information.
- Uses figurative language to compare or to enhance understanding in some way
- Departs from the narrative to explain (a concept important to understanding the narrative).

FIGURE 6.1. Language for describing types of details in (but not limited to) narrative texts.

sentence aloud, thinking about specific details in the sentence, and annotating your thoughts.

During lessons, regardless of the grade level I am teaching, I always project the text in some way for all students to view. Before I ask students to read and annotate a text, I help them get started by modeling how I decide to write particular annotations in the margins of the text. My annotations are clearly related to the purpose for close reading; I even think aloud, "Now when I think about what the author has written *and* my purpose for close reading . . ." So if the purpose for close reading is "How does the author develop the idea that cell phones might be harmful?" then I think aloud like this and write annotations (mostly) related to this purpose. Based on my observation of the students, I then begin a shared think-aloud and shared writing of notes; I elicit their thoughts and together we decide what to write in the margins of the text. Figure 6.2 shows the excerpt of a text from *Marching for Freedom* (Partridge, 2009) with annotations I made during a think-aloud; the excerpt was projected on the document camera for the whole class to view as I engaged in a think-aloud and write-aloud of annotations.

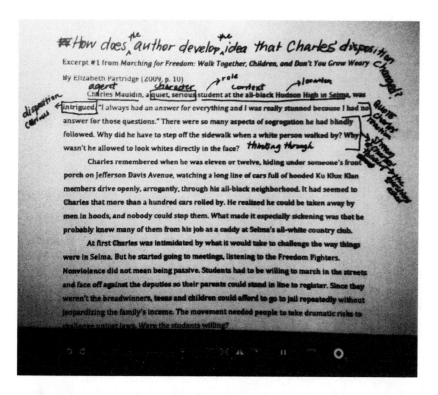

FIGURE 6.2. Annotated text projected on the document camera.

Use the Concept of *Author's Craft* as a Lens for Examining Details

There are many definitions for the term *author's craft*. Generally, when this term is used in an English language arts classroom, teachers are referring to the literary techniques or devices an author uses to convey a message. These devices include *foreshadowing, backstory,* and *flashback*. While planning lessons for a group of middle school students, the teachers and I started pondering if we could use this term—*author's craft*—with their students. The students were familiar with this concept as it applied to fictional narratives so we decided to see how they used it to think about nonfiction narratives.

With a class of seventh-grade students, we engaged in close reading of the two passages (discussed early in this chapter) about the youth who were involved in the voting rights marches in Selma, Alabama, in 1964. Figure 6.3 illustrates the purpose for close reading that I posted. Together the class and I generated a list of types of details and the students also took notes to reference as they worked independently. The students clearly tapped their understanding of the author's craft as it relates to fictional narrative texts when they identified the details. For

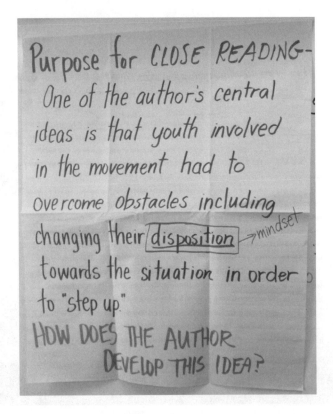

FIGURE 6.3. Purpose for close reading of excerpt from *Marching for Freedom* (Partridge, 2009).

example, when we read about Charles's experience with the Ku Klux Klan, one student's hand shot up and he couldn't help but yell, "That's a flashback!" I had not thought of calling Charles's experience a flashback, but realized it was an appropriate term. I took advantage of this moment to annotate my copy of the text on the document camera, writing the word *flashback* in the margin and adding this term to our list.

Model How to Use Annotated Notes to Engage in Small-Group Conversations

As a teacher, I seldom call on individual students to share aloud. Mostly I ask students to turn and talk with a partner (see Figure 6.4), and then I sit in on conversations and coach them to listen and respond in ways that add meaning. Often I have to model this activity for students as well. I start by asking a volunteer to have a conversation with me in front of the class. The annotated excerpt we created together during the shared think-aloud is projected on the document camera, and I remind the individual who volunteered to bring his or her notes, too. Then I model how to start a conversation about the content I learned from a text excerpt and anything else I learned based on our purpose for close reading. I point to the notes I am referring to as I speak. At a certain point I stop and ask the student volunteer to carry on, and I prompt him or her to refer to his or her

FIGURE 6.4. A second-grade student explains to a peer how she used the details in the excerpt to draw an illustration.

notes. I explicitly review what the student volunteer and I did as we engaged in conversation, including the following points:

- We revisited the purpose for close reading to make sure our conversation was on topic.
- We used our notes as a reference to summarize the content and how the author developed this content.
- We cited the text when we needed to support our points.
- We asked each other questions when we did not understand.

At first this approach may lead to very shallow conversations, but it is possible to "up the ante." You can give students prompts that require critical thinking, such as, "What is the value of this particular kind of detail [or of this technique] the author has employed?" Questions related to the content are also important: "What do you understand now about the obstacles youth had to face in order to join this movement? How does empathy deepen your understanding of what they faced?"

CHAPTER SEVEN

Why Pay Attention to Connective Language?

Words and phrases, called *connectives* (Crosson & Lesaux, 2013), provide opportunities for an author to link ideas in a text. The presence and role of connectives contribute to the complexity of a text. Let's consider the connectives in an excerpt from *Marching from Freedom: Walk Together, Children, and Don't You Grow Weary* (Partridge, 2009). As noted in previous chapters, the author's purpose in this text as a whole is to tell the story of how youth were involved in the civil rights marches that led to President Lyndon Johnson's signing of the Voting Rights Act in 1965. Partridge employs a narrative structure to serve her purpose. In the first chapter, she tells the story of how one civil rights activist, Amelia Boynton, worked tirelessly to help African American voters in Dallas County, Alabama, register to vote. In the following paragraph, Partridge makes the point that even though Boynton had endeavored to help more people register to vote, there was still only a fraction of the county's African American population registered. Take a moment to consider how the phrase "but despite" (in **bold** for the purposes of this example) reveals the relationship between these ideas.

> Selma, the seat of Dallas County, had a population of 30,000 and was more than half black. **But despite** Mrs. Boynton's efforts, 99 percent of the voters were white. (p. 2)

Partridge is signaling that the low number of registered African American voters was a huge problem and remained a persistent problem *despite, contrary to* the efforts of activists such as Boynton to increase their numbers. The phrase "but despite" creates an adversative relationship between two ideas: (1) Mrs. Boynton's efforts (named in the second sentence and described in the previous paragraph) and (2) the persistently low number of African American voters in Dallas County (an inference made from analysis of content in the first and second sentences).

So the phrase "but despite" connects two ideas, and it also serves as an impetus for the importance of another idea that is introduced just a bit later in the text. Mrs. Boynton recognized the continued problem and was not going to give up her pursuit. Her persistence led her to recruit Dr. King and the Southern Christian Leadership Conference to come to Selma. In the end, enlisting their support would be a key move in getting the Voting Rights Act passed.

There are many categories of connectors. In this chapter, I discuss four major categories:

1. Additive
2. Temporal
3. Causal
4. Adversative

In the discussion following each category of connectives, I share examples from authentic texts and explain the function of the connectives in these particular passages. A list of the connectives is presented in Figure 7.1.

Additive Connectives

Additive connectives are words or phrases that add one idea to another, without a causal relationship. Two or more ideas added together by connectives may add weight or a sense of urgency to an idea, thus improving the general quality of a larger idea. Some examples of additive connectives are:

also	*such as*	*and*
furthermore	*as well*	*moreover*
besides	*what is more*	*in addition*

In *Marching to the Mountaintop: How Poverty, Labor Fights, and Civil Rights Set the Stage for Martin Luther King, Jr.'s Final Hours* (Bausum, 2012), the author describes the political context in 1968 for the sanitation workers who went on strike in Memphis, Tennessee. The city government was largely ineffective in responding to the crisis of accumulating garbage in the streets. In this passage, notice Bausum's use of the connective *and* (in **bold** to highlight our purpose):

> Members of the city council struggled to find their roles in the growing crisis. Like the mayor, they were new to their jobs **and** to a weeks-old governance system. The

---

Additive Connectives

Additive connectives are words or phrases that add one idea to another. There is no causal relationship between ideas. The ideas together, though, may improve the general quality of a larger idea, including adding weight or a sense of urgency to an idea.

also	*such as*	*and*
furthermore	*as well*	*moreover*
besides	*what is more*	*in addition*

Temporal Connectives

Temporal connectives signal a relationship in time between ideas.

by then	*(just) before*	*after*
until	*meanwhile*	*in the meantime*
eventually	*subsequently*	

Causal Connectives

The language of this type of connective signals a causal relationship between two ideas. *Although some connectives are temporal, their importance is in how they also signal causal relationships between ideas.

because	*as a result*	*therefore*
thus	*consequently*	*hence*
so	*until*	*if . . . (then)*
that's why		
*when	**after*	**as soon as*

Adversative Connectives

Adversative connectives signal a causal relationship that is in opposition or contrary to what would have been expected.

but	*notwithstanding*	*however*
even though	*although*	*yet*
despite	*in contrast*	*while*
whereas	*instead*	*nevertheless*

FIGURE 7.1. Examples of connectives.

mayor insisted that he alone could negotiate on behalf of the city, **and** he became angry whenever council members tried to settle the strike. The ten whites on the council (including the council's sole female member) saw little reason to challenge his authority, **and** the three blacks on the council lacked the political power to argue otherwise. (p. 29)

In this passage, Bausum describes what seems like insurmountable circumstances. The connective "and," used three times, serves to *add on to* or build a cumulative problem. The problem was not just that the members were new to their jobs; they were *also* new to the crisis and were *also* working with a volatile mayor and *also* lacked political motivation and power. Again, the sum of these factors is greater than each of them alone.

Consider the function of the connective *in addition to* (in **bold** for our purposes) in this passage from Murphy's (2010) *The Great Fire*:

> The Tribune Building was one of the newer "fireproof" structures, one which, for many citizens, symbolized the wealth and energy of Chicago. **In addition to** a granite-block exterior, the interior ceilings were of corrugated iron, resting upon wrought iron I beams, and every partition wall in the structure was of brick. It was in all respects, one of the most absolutely fireproof buildings ever erected. (p. 73)

Murphy is listing the features of this building, but his use of "in addition to" creates a *sum* of the features. He is trying to convey that, somehow, it was not just one feature that made this building "absolutely fireproof" but the sum of all of these features. The sentence would have a different effect if Murphy simply had written:

> This building had a granite-block exterior, interior ceilings were of corrugated iron resting upon wrought iron I beams, and every partition wall in the structure was of brick.

Temporal Connectives

Temporal connectives signal a relationship in time between ideas. Some examples of temporal connectives are:

by then	*(just) before*	*after*
until	*meanwhile*	*in the meantime*
eventually	*subsequently*	

Notice the temporal connectives (in **bold** for our purposes) in this passage from *A Drop of Water* (Wick, 1997):

> The drop grows heavy and **begins** to fall. **As** it breaks from a strand of water, the drop shrinks itself into a round ball, or sphere. The drop flattens **then** elongates **as** it falls. The strand, **meanwhile**, breaks into tiny droplets. (p. 8)

Four different connectives are used in this excerpt. *Merriam-Webster.com* (n.d.) defines them as follows:

- *Begins*—"to proceed to perform the first or earliest part of some action."
- *As*—"at the same time that."
- *Then*—"next in order of time."
- *Meanwhile*—also "at the same time."

In this paragraph, the reader has to create an image of a sequence—a drop of water starting to fall, breaking from a strand of water, becoming a sphere, and then flattening and lengthening at the same time that it is falling through the air. How do we know this is happening in this sequence? Because of the connectives *begins, as,* and *then.* These words have signaled a series of events. But then another series of events is happening at the same time: Water droplets continue to drop from the strand. How do we know the events are occurring simultaneously? We know this because of the connective *meanwhile.*

An author's use of connectives depends on his or her purpose. In *A Drop of Water* (Wick, 1997), the author wants to explain what happens when a droplet separates from a strand of water. He uses connectives to establish an order of events. Contrast this with Hague's (2012) use of temporal connectives in the first chapter of *Alien Deep.* As described in a previous chapter, the purpose of this book is to describe hydrothermal vents and explain their effect on the sea floor landscape. Hague begins this chapter by narrating the discovery, on February 15, 1977, of a hydrothermal vent on the ocean floor; he identifies this event as a "scientific revolution" (p. 9). I have selected two sentences from consecutive paragraphs about midway through this chapter. Notice the temporal connectives he uses (in bold for our purpose):

1. **Today**, we know that Earth's crust is broken into great slabs called plates that travel across the planet's surface as though on some sort of slow-moving conveyor belt.
2. **Back in the 1970's**, though, this idea was still in its infancy, and the biggest question was what powered this "belt."

Hague is using connective language—*today* and *back in the 1970's*—to develop the idea that scientists know more today than they did decades ago. If you read the rest of the chapter, you might notice that he continues to use connectives (temporal and causal) to develop the idea that since the first discovery of a hydrothermal vent on February 15, 1977, scientists have revised what they thought they knew about the sea floor landscape and the geology of the Earth. They have learned a tremendous amount through continued research. Yet, as Hague states in the last paragraph of this chapter, "The quest to understand the deep ocean is **just beginning**" (p. 15). While Wick uses temporal connectives to describe a sequence of events, Hague uses temporal connectives (as well as anecdotes about past research expeditions, descriptions of hydrothermal vents and plate tectonics, and the language of causal connectives) to create a conceptual understanding of scientific practice: how scientists are always conducting research, asking questions, and learning from their research. They did this in the past, they do so in the present, and they will continue to do so in the future. This usage serves to inform the reader of Hague's purpose and sets the tone for the book.

Causal Connectives

This type of connective signals a causal relationship between two ideas. Examples of causal connectives are:

because	*as a result*	*therefore*
thus	*consequently*	*hence*
so	*until*	*if . . . (then)*
that's why	*when*	

In Wick's (1997) text *A Drop of Water*, "When Water Flows Up" includes a photograph of water flowing up glass tubes. In the excerpt below, Wick uses connectives (in **bold** for our purposes) to cue the reader to causal relationships.

> Water molecules cling to materials such as glass with an attractive force called adhesion. **That's why** water drops cling to windowpanes after a rain. This attraction also **causes** water to creep up the sides of the glass tubes. The narrower the tube, the higher the water will climb. (p. 13)

In the second and third sentences, Wick clearly cues the reader to the causal relationships with the connectives *that's why* and *causes*. However, he does not always do this. In the last sentence, the reader has to infer that the width of the glass tube (cause) and adhesion (cause) make the water climb higher (effect) than in tubes of narrower widths.

Some causal relationships are disguised by connectives that appear to be temporal. Although the relationship may *appear* to have a time–order relation, the important point is the causal relation. Examples of (sometimes) disguised causal connectives are:

when	*after*	*as soon as*

Notice the use of *when* (in **bold** for our purposes) in the following excerpt from *Volcanoes* (Murray, 1996):

> **When** crustal plates pull apart or crash against each other, we can feel the earth shift beneath our feet. (p. 10)

Although *when* can signal a temporal order, in this case, what is more important is the causal relationship. The focus is not on *when*, as in tomorrow or next week, but on crustal plates causing the earth to shift.

Adversative Connectives

Adversative connectives signal a causal relationship that is in opposition or contrary to what would have been expected. Earlier in this chapter, I explained the adversative connective in the excerpt from *Marching for Freedom* (Partridge, 2009). Based on Mrs. Boynton's tireless efforts to increase the number of African Americans registered to vote in Dallas County, Alabama, you would *not* expect the numbers of those actually registered to remain so low. The adversative connective *but despite,* along with the contraposition of statistics about the number of African Americans in Dallas County and the number registered to vote, plays a huge role in conveying Partridge's idea that this is a problem. Examples of adversative connectives include:

but	*notwithstanding*	*however*
even though	*although*	*yet*
despite	*in contrast*	*while*
whereas	*instead*	*nevertheless*

Consider this passage from *The Triangle Shirtwaist Factory Fire* (Nobleman, 2008), part of the Compass Point Books *We the People* series:

> Employees were afraid to speak out against the dangerous work conditions in these factories, known as sweat shops, because the bosses would not hesitate to fire troublemakers. Finding another job could take a while, during which time they would have no income. Besides, most of the workers knew that the conditions at other factories were no better. (p. 12)
>
> **Yet** the workers had power as a group. (p. 13)

In this passage, the meaning of the word *yet* (in **bold** for our purposes) is *still* or *nevertheless*. There is so much power in the meaning of this word. Here,

Nobleman, the author, is turning the situation upside down. Just when you think there's no hope for these workers, with the connective *yet* there is suddenly hope. This connective links the idea of no hope to some hope, and, as a result, moves the reader forward.

Recommendations for Instruction

Define Connectives for Yourself to Create Clarity for Your Students

Connectives are a unique domain of vocabulary that may be overlooked by student readers. Even when students do recognize a connective such as *but*, they may not have the language needed to describe how this word serves to reveal relationships between ideas, and how it might add to the logical development of an author's ideas. How do you define *but, besides, furthermore?* I have started working on how I articulate the meanings of these words—taking into account the context in which they are used in a particular text. When planning lessons, I look up the definitions of these words to nurture my own ability to explain the meanings to students. My best resources are online dictionaries. I surf through definitions, picking and choosing words and phrases based on the needs of the students I am teaching. What words and phrases will provide clarity for the students regarding the meaning of a particular connective as it is used in a particular text?

Address Connectives during Close Reading Instruction

I do not isolate teaching connectives from working with high-quality texts and (when possible) as part of reading texts related to an integrated unit of study. During close reading with students, I identify and define connectives for students as a way to deepen their understanding of the relationship of the ideas in the text. For example, during a lesson with seventh graders, I used two short excerpts from *Marching for Freedom* (Partridge, 2009) to highlight the personal obstacles these youth had to face to join the civil rights movement. In one excerpt about Charles Mauldin, we read the following two sentences:

> At first Charles was intimidated by what it would take to challenge the way things were in Selma. But he started going to meetings, listening to the Freedom Fighters. (p.10)

On my copy of the excerpt placed under the document camera, I put a box around the word *but* and stopped to discuss the role of this word—how it means that the author is going to share a "contrasting idea." I modeled thinking aloud about how the idea of Charles being intimidated contrasts with his confronting his

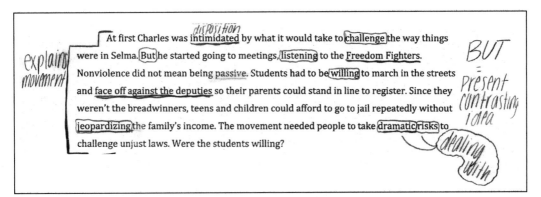

FIGURE 7.2. A student's annotated excerpt from *Marching for Freedom* (Partridge, 2009).

fears by attending meetings of the Freedom Fighters. Several students noted this contrast in their annotations. (See Figure 7.2 for one example.)

During a second-grade lesson, I worked with a group of students in closely reading an excerpt from a descriptive text about the aye-aye, a type of lemur native to Madagascar. Here are the first three sentences of the passage:

> Aye-ayes sleep in nests in the highest trees of the rainforest. But they don't sleep at night. The aye-aye is a nocturnal animal. It is active at night and sleeps all day. (Robinson, 2013, p. 5)

With this passage on the smart board, I put a box around the word *but*. The sentence "But they don't sleep at night" contrasts with what the reader has experienced—that most animals sleep at night and are awake during the day. There is no sentence prior to this one with a contrasting idea. The reader has to create this contrast for herself or identify that she is confused and continue reading to discover that the author has explained his point further in the next two sentences. The students grasped this as I held a brief discussion about why the author used the word *but* and then moved on.

Figures 7.3 and 7.4 show anchor charts I used during a lesson with sixth-grade students. Notice how I highlight "in spite of" in the two images. The first is a definition of *perseverant* and the second was our purpose for close reading. During the lesson I focused on how this phrase is an adversative connective, which means that one idea or factor did not influence the outcome of the situation. Again, my purpose was to draw awareness to this phrase and how it plays an important role both in the prompt and in our thinking through the central ideas of a text while doing close reading.

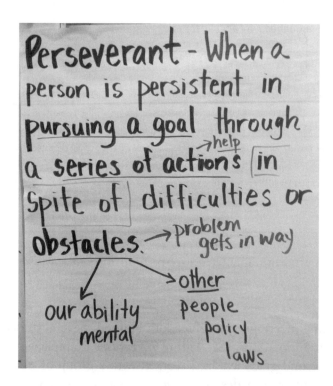

FIGURE 7.3. Anchor chart with a definition of *perseverant.*

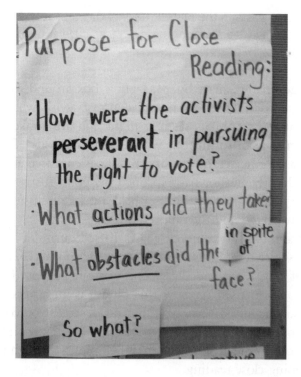

FIGURE 7.4. Anchor chart with the purpose for close reading.

CHAPTER EIGHT

How Are Main Ideas Constructed?

In Chapter One we examined the difference between an author's purpose and the main ideas in a text. To reiterate, an author has a purpose or purposes for writing a text before he or she begins developing the text itself. The author's purpose may or may not be explicitly stated in a text, and the reader may have to infer it by asking questions related to the five purposes explained in Chapter Two:

"Is the author describing his or her topic to me, the reader?"

"Is the author explaining how something happens?"

"Is the author providing procedures or instructions to enable me to do something?"

"Is the author trying to persuade me?"

"Is the author telling the story of a particular event or group?"

Unlike these purposes, the author's main ideas do not fit neatly into categories. Instead they place a larger demand on the reader to tap life experiences and prior knowledge from an array of content-area subjects and ways of thinking.

Gist, Theme, and Topic

As stated previously, a *main idea* is a broad term that has been interpreted in many ways. In this book, I address main ideas at the gist level and the theme level, as defined below:

- The **gist** is a short summary with content specific to a particular text that also conveys a bigger idea or important point in the whole text or a section of the text.
- The **theme** of a text is a global idea that can be applied to the text in hand as well as other texts.

In Chapter Two, I compared the gist and themes in *What Bluebirds Do* (Kirby 2009) and in *Bootleg* (Blumenthal, 2011). (See Table 2.1 on page 15 for more details.) In Table 8.1 I have done this again for two additional texts—*Sit-In: How Four Friends Stood Up By Sitting Down* (Pinkney, 2010) and a Science News for Students article *Aquatic Predators Affect Carbon-Storing Plant Life* (Raloff, 2013).

TABLE 8.1. Purpose, Gist, and Theme

Term	Definition of term	*Sit-In: How Four Friends Stood Up by Sitting Down* (Pinkney, 2010)	*Aquatic Predators Affect Carbon-Storing Plant Life* (Raloff, 2013)
Purpose	The purpose is the reason why a text is written: to provide instructions, to recount, to describe, to explain, to persuade.	The author's purpose for this text is to narrate or tell the story of four African American men who refused to give up their seats at a segregated lunch counter even when they were verbally and physically abused.	The author's purpose is to explain the effects of removing top predators from freshwater environments.
Gist	The gist of a text is a very short summary that also conveys a bigger idea or main point in the text.	One gist is: During the Civil Rights Movement, a group of social activists, who believed segregation was an injustice, courageously refused to give up their seats at a segregated Woolworth lunch counter. They persevered despite being antagonized.	One gist is: Research is revealing that in freshwater environments, when top predators die off due to human impact, zoo plankton (normally eaten by those top predators) flourish and over feed on carbon-reducing algae. This, in turn, increases the amount of carbon dioxide in the water and in the atmosphere with potentially disastrous effects.
Theme	The theme of a text is a global idea that can be applied to the text in hand.	Perseverance is an important attribute of effective civil rights movements. One group's courage can inspire another group to join a cause and take action.	Human damage to the environment may have disastrous effects for an ecosystem.

In the picture book *Sit-In: How Four Friends Stood Up By Sitting Down* (Pinkney, 2010), the author's purpose is to tell the story of four African American college students who decided to protest the injustices of segregation by refusing to give up seats in the "Whites Only" section of the local Woolworth's lunch counter. Pinkney also describes the effects of this courageous endeavor, including other students leading sit-ins across the segregated south, the boycott of businesses that practiced segregation, the decision by businesses to survive by segregating, and the eventual signing of the Civil Rights Act by President Johnson in 1964. There are many main ideas that can be gleaned from this text—at the gist and theme levels. Vocabulary like *perseverance, courage, collaboration, leadership, hope,* and *unity* can be integrated into statements at both idea levels.

In the Science News for Students article *Aquatic Predators Affect Carbon-Storing Plant Life* (Raloff, 2013), the author's purpose is to explain what happens when top predators in freshwater environments die off owing to human activity like pesticide run off. Raloff details the specifics of a research study revealing that when top predators in this ecosystem die, their prey—zoo plankton—overfeeds on carbon algae. This result is disastrous for the ecosystem because the algae, which are photosynthetic organisms, store and use carbon. When they do so, more carbon dioxide is drawn from the atmosphere—which helps humans survive. When the algae are not present, the amount of carbon dioxide in the water increases and less is drawn from the atmosphere; the implication is calamitous. A simple gist for this article is "research reveals top predators are crucial to a freshwater ecosystem's survival." A more complex gist would integrate information about the role of top predators in the ecosystem and the effects that occur when these predators disappear.

A gist statement and a theme statement can overlap in content, conveying nearly the same message. For example, in Table 8.1 for *Sit-In: How Four Friends Stood Up By Sitting Down* (Pinkney, 2010), I used the vocabulary word *perseverance* in both statements. While the gist statement is about one group of activists in particular, the theme statement is broader and can be applied to thinking about other texts and contexts.

For some informational texts, particularly non-narrative texts, a gist or theme might be difficult to derive. Consider the text *Frogs* (Bishop, 2008). Traditionally, the focus of a reader might be on the *topic* of this text stated as "frogs" or "all about frogs" or "frogs' physical attributes and how they survive." It is more of a leap (no pun intended), for a reader to identify a gist or a theme. A *gist* for this text might be the following:

Frogs are a diverse group of animals with a variety of features that contribute to their survival.

The difference between the suggested topics and the stated gist is a degree of meaning. The topic is basically a word or phrase *labeling* the subject of the text or section of text (Cunningham & Moore, 1986). In the gist statement, the words and phrases "diverse," "variety," and "contribute to" deepen the meaning of what is being said. A theme for *Frogs* might be:

Living things have a variety of physical features that contribute to their survival.

This theme is helpful to consider if the reader is reading multiple texts about living things or animals and plants. Again, there is a difference in degree of meaning and even utility in thinking about a gist versus a theme. The theme is global and can be used as a lens for thinking about other texts.

Relationships between Ideas Reveal the Main Idea

Constructing a main idea is about noticing the relationships between ideas in a text. The "how" of a text—its complexity and the way its many parts work together—cues us to the relationship between ideas. Knowing an author's purpose gives the reader a clue about what to pay attention to as important in a text. Being aware of the structure and the author's use of connectives helps the reader follow the author's logic and development of ideas. Naming the types of details aids the reader in categorizing ideas, noticing repetition and overlap, and signaling importance. And the list goes on.

Let's consider how *constructing a main idea by noticing relationships between ideas* works with a particular text. Throughout *Marching for Freedom: Walk Together, Children, and Don't You Grow Weary* (Partridge, 2009) (described in previous chapters), there are multiple events that occur over the course of the book that reveal how the activists faced particular obstacles, overcame those obstacles, and continued in pursuit of their goal of voting rights. These include the following:

- In Dallas County, Alabama, Sandra Boynton tries to help more African Americans register to vote, but the numbers of registered voters remain low because blacks are intimidated and fearful. As a result, she recruits Dr. Martin Luther King, Jr., and his organization, the Southern Christian Leadership Conference (SCLC) to come to Selma and help.
- Local youth began to join the SCLC's movement, but they faced inner obstacles—fear and their own ignorance about how life might be different than life under segregation. And yet, young adults like Charles Mauldin

overcame these personal obstacles and began to act as leaders in the movement.

- On March 7th, hundreds of youth and adults started a march from Selma
to Montgomery, the capital of Alabama. They were blocked by police on
horses and then attacked in what would be called "Bloody Sunday." They
regrouped and continued the march on March 21, this time with the pro-
tection of the Alabama National Guard.

Over and over again, Partridge describes how the activists faced problems or
obstacles, but did not let this get in the way of pursuing the right to vote. The
sum of these incidents is *perseverance* or the quality of being persistent in pursuing
a goal through a series of actions in spite of difficulties or obstacles. As readers
begin to realize how the incidents being presented by Partridge are related, they
can draw from their understanding of main ideas, including their knowledge of
theme vocabulary (described later in this chapter).

Even in short texts or text excerpts, the relationship between ideas can reveal
a main idea. Reconsider the one-paragraph excerpt in the Introduction from
Bones: Our Skeletal System (Simon, 2000). Simon begins by naming a part of the
system: the backbone. Next he zooms in to name and describe the parts of the
backbone, the vertebrae, and the joints between each vertebra. Finally he zooms
back out again to the spine and its function: it lets you bend down to touch your
toes but keeps your body upright, not allowing it to just flop over. If a reader
recognizes the relationship between the ideas at the beginning, middle, and ending of this one paragraph, this recognition can aid the reader in articulating the
gist—the backbone is a system of purposefully organized parts—the vertebrae—
that, together, allows our bodies to function in a critical way.

Most Main Ideas Are Not Stated Clearly
in a "Main Idea Sentence"

Some authors explicitly state main ideas at the gist or theme level, but many do
not. Let's consider a case study of main ideas in three articles in one issue of
National Geographic Explorer! Pathfinder Edition (2012) geared toward an audience of fluent readers in fourth and fifth grades. Remember, these are the main
ideas that emerged for me, "the expert reader," but because the ideas are textually
supported, other readers should notice them as well.

In the first article, "Got Poison?" (Wedner, 2012), the author identifies four
key ideas early in the article, but not in one "main idea" sentence. At the beginning of the article, the author introduces the context with a description of a
nighttime scenario when a viper catches a bat and kills it with deadly poison.

(By the way, this introduction is much more engaging than my summary of it!) The first section of the text, "Poison Power" (which follows the introduction), includes the main ideas of the article, each stated in the first sentence of three separate paragraphs. I've listed the first sentences of each of the three paragraphs (p. 4) below. Notice their potential as key ideas in the article.

1. Using poisons helps them [a variety of snakes] survive.
2. Toxins, or chemicals in these poisons, work in many different ways.
3. Animals also have different ways of spreading their poisons.

After the first sentence in each paragraph, the author consistently gives examples of the idea stated. For example, she describes and names other animals that "use poison power to survive." Later in the article, text features such as the subheading "Stings and Stabs" (how poison is spread) and the caption "This Komodo dragon's drippy saliva can be poisonous" continue to cue the reader to the main idea that "animals have different ways of spreading their poisons." As the reader reads the extended prose in the article, she might notice the similarity in details employed by the author to reinforce the ideas stated in the main-idea sentences above. So, did the author explicitly state the main idea? No. Did she give some hefty clues? Yes. In the end, the reader still has to engage in some construction of the gist of the text.

In the second article, "In the Strike Zone" (Samaras, 2012), the author's first paragraph gives a general (not very helpful) idea of what may become important.

My team and I are storm chasers. We look for lightning so we can study it. Chasing lightning is pretty exciting. Why don't you come along and see for yourself. (p. 12)

The reader might think that "so we can study it" is the main idea of the article, but the author never describes "studying lightning"—only the equipment the team uses to locate lightning and how they use vehicles to escape dangerous situations. There is no explanation of how they learn about lightning. Most of the article's content is about how lightning works and its physical attributes. The "storm chasing" is primarily a narrative frame for the content.

The reader might also think that "lightning is pretty exciting" is a main idea sentence, but this is too general to be of much help in determining what is contextually important. This sentence lends itself to a situation in which the reader responds solely on affect, thinking "Do *I* think this is pretty exciting?"

My interpretation of this article's main ideas is that the author wants to convey that lightning is an interesting phenomenon, that we know a lot about it, and that it is studied by people who do this for a living because there is even more to learn about this phenomenon. In the end, this is a well-written article that students should read, but its main idea is not explicitly stated.

In the third article, entitled "Super Survivors" (Miller, 2012), what seems to be a main idea statement, in the first paragraph of the text, is actually misleading.

> Sunlight shines down onto a swamp. The ground is wet and spongy. The air is hot and humid. This may seem like a great habitat for plants. Yet many plants here struggle. They simply can't get everything they need to survive. (p. 18)

The reader might think that "many plants here struggle" or "can't get everything they need to survive" is the main idea —but it's not. Actually, the plants described in the article, such as the sundew plant and dragon's blood tree, survive just fine. In fact, the main idea is that some plants survive differently because their habitat lacks what other plants need to thrive. The author never states this idea, but he does scaffold the reader for inferring it. For example, he includes a strong first paragraph in each section, such as the following under the subheading "Seaweed in the Desert":

> Few plants can live in a desert. It's too dry there. Yet the desert seaweed grows well in the African desert. (p. 21)

A textually based main idea may emerge if the reader is able to:

- Predict the author's purpose of explaining how plants survive (which is heavily scaffolded for, beginning with the article's title, "Super Survivors").
- Understand enumerative structure and identify that the author focuses on different aspects of how plants survive in nutrient-poor habitats.
- Follow the author's logic by noticing connectives such as *yet* in this example above.
- Notice (while unpacking sentences dense with content) the similarities in the details shared, such as specific names of plants, where they grow, and how they survive in harsh habitats.

My point is that main ideas are not always explicitly stated. In fact, in my experience reading informational texts, main ideas are *rarely* stated explicitly. Instead the reader has to *construct* this idea for himself as he reads further and even rereads a text multiple times. Yet the reader is not alone. Reading an informational text is a transactional experience between the reader and the author and text. The complexities of the text—the multiple dimensions discussed in this book and how they fit and work together—serve the reader in noticing relationships and, from this, gleaning main ideas.

Main Idea Vocabulary

Most of this book has focused on the informational text itself: how it is constructed and the language related to articulating this *how*. The concept of *main ideas* is abstract compared with the concepts of *text structure* or *connectives* or *types of details*. The concept is harder to generalize since there are no neat sets of main ideas for readers to reference. Instead, the reader has to use a large array of vocabulary from many domains to interpret and then explain a main idea. Because main ideas are not explicitly stated in many texts, the onus falls on the reader to draw from this repertoire of vocabulary.

For many years in my work with students, I have felt an overwhelming lack of vocabulary knowledge that students can tap and use to explain main ideas in complex texts. Many times, as educators, we jump straight from reading the text to asking students, "What is the main idea?" without first engaging them in experiences that let them grapple with the meaning of already-stated main ideas. In other words, students need opportunities to think about main ideas that include vocabulary such as *courage, perseverance,* and *humanitarianism* before they are asked to identify main ideas on their own.

I have also found that students' knowledge of vocabulary is superficial. For example, one student might say that to be *courageous* means "to be brave." Here, she has substituted one word for another without really explaining the meaning. Students are less likely to state that courageous means "the ability to do something you know is difficult or dangerous" (*Merriam-Webster.com*, 2014). They are even less likely to explain the term further by saying that courage includes "the mental or moral strength to venture, persevere, and withstand danger, fear, or difficulty." This expanded meaning is important for students to understand when they read about a historical figure who had to take initial steps in the face of obstacles, persist until a goal or outcome was met, and stayed safe along the way.

This complex definition of the word *courage* provides more content for students to use when explaining their interpretations of main ideas in a text. Many students can easily say, "This person was courageous." And many students can give supporting evidence from the text: "This person did *X, X,* and *X.*" Where the students stumble is in their explanation of the evidence, perhaps because they cannot articulate the dimensions of the word *courage* beyond "it means brave." But what if a student understood that courage is doing something difficult, dangerous, something you fear? And that courage is not always something that happens in one moment (e.g., pushing someone out of the way of a bullet), but a state of mind that has to be sustained over time to accomplish a goal?

My work with main-idea vocabulary is heavily influenced by Beck, McKeown, and Kucan's (2013) classic text *Bringing Words to Life: Robust Vocabulary Instruction.* Basically, main idea vocabulary is what these authors would term "Tier Two" vocabulary, or words that can be used in many domains. Figure 8.1 includes a list of vocabulary words and phrases that might be helpful to students in identifying and explaining main ideas. Although teachers may be tempted to give lists of words to students, I argue instead for engaging in narrowly focused, in-depth conversations on particular words with multiple texts. Often what we identify as students' "lack of vocabulary" is also their "superficial understanding of vocabulary." In the rest of this chapter, I describe lessons I experienced with students and make the case for why we need to teach vocabulary as part of thematic units of study with informational text sets.

Recommendations for Instruction

Teach and Observe—and Teach Again—for Deep Understanding of Theme Words

In my work in a large urban school district, I had the privilege of teaching a class of sixth-grade students. Their teacher plans her units of study using Wiggins and McTighe's (2005) *Understanding by Design*, an approach we might call *backward*

• Ability to overcome obstacles • Capacity • Change, process, metamorphosis, innovation, transformation • Circle of life • Collective wisdom • Communication • Community • Compassion, benevolence, empathy • Cooperation • Courage, endurance, determination, enterprise • Curiosity	• Dangers of ignorance • Destruction • Displacement • Discovery • Diversity, complexity • Education • Empowerment • Essentiality • Fear, trepidation, reverence • Friendship, alliance, harmony, solidarity • Global citizenship • Hope • Humanitarianism • Injustice, tyranny	• Instigation, agitation, disturbance, perturbation, provocation, invincibility • Knowledge versus ignorance • Nonviolent, peaceful, placid, amicable • Oppression • Perseverance, tenacity • Power • Progress, breakthrough, momentum • Rebirth, renewal, restoration • Resilience • Survival • Vulnerability

• Complexity and diversity of living organisms
• Essential role of *X* in the system of *X*
• Similarities/differences between concept *A* and concept *B* (and why it is important to understand how they contrast)
• Making the unfamiliar (or the feared) more familiar (and less feared)
• Information or details about *X* presented in such a way as to transform our thinking

FIGURE 8.1. Some main or central idea vocabulary for informational texts.

planning. She begins by choosing the themes for a unit of study and then, with this in mind, chooses texts that scaffold for understanding of the theme. When I visited her classroom to teach, her students were engaged in a unit of study entitled "Exploring Resistance and Struggle throughout Varied Cultures."

I visited the teacher a few weeks before she started this unit, and we looked at her students' writing in response to a text for another unit, this one examining the dimensions of the Cherokee culture. We noticed that many students used vocabulary words such as *respect* to make a claim and attempted to supply evidence to support it. What was not clear was their understanding of these words. Do they know that when you respect someone, you understand this person's importance or value in a particular context? In a sense, the students were grappling with words such as *respect* and offering evidence, but a solid explanation of the vocabulary word they had chosen and how the evidence revealed this was missing. This was a trend for many of the student essays we analyzed. Students used Tier Two vocabulary to identify main ideas, but they did not articulate the meaning of those words and did not explain how the evidence they provided illustrated the main idea.

Based on our formative assessment of the students' writing, we decided to plan a lesson focused on helping them articulate the meaning of one word: *perseverance.* We would engage the students in a close reading of an excerpt from *Marching for Freedom: Walk Together, Children, and Don't You Grow Weary* (Partridge, 2009). We chose the vocabulary word, the text, and the instructional approach to align with the unit of study on struggle and resistance, but kept students' needs in mind. Figure 8.2 shows a lesson plan template for this and similar lessons that focus on introducing vocabulary and the main idea of an excerpt before engaging in close reading for the purposes of identifying and explaining supporting evidence.

The excerpt for this lesson was from the first chapter of *Marching for Freedom* when Partridge (2009) introduces the reader to Sandra Boynton, a civil rights activist in Selma, Alabama, who had repeatedly attempted to register African Americans in Dallas County to vote. As described earlier in this chapter, her efforts were nearly futile, and the number of registered blacks remained small. Boynton did not give up, though. She was *perseverant,* recruiting college students to help her register voters, and then finally driving to Atlanta and recruiting Dr. King and his organization, the Southern Christian Leadership Conference, to come to Selma and march for voting rights. (At the very beginning of this lesson, I read aloud the first few pages from this text to the students to attract their interest. Using the document camera, I also showed them the primary sources and photographs that Partridge included on these pages.)

In brief, the lesson plan involved introducing the students to the word *perseverant* and then reading and rereading the excerpt with the following prompt:

Objectives of Lesson
- Students will understand a key vocabulary word (e.g., *courage, perseverance, investigate*) that can be used to identify the main or central idea of a passage.
- Students will engage in close reading to identify supporting evidence for the main or central idea and explain this evidence both orally and in writing.

Preparation and Materials
- Study the excerpt, underline key words and phrases, and annotate *only* in relation to the purpose for close reading.
- Create an anchor chart with the *vocabulary word* defined in large, clear print.
- Create an anchor chart with the *purpose for close reading* clearly stated as a question (e.g., "How did the civil rights activists practice perseverance?" or "How did the scientist engage in investigation?").
- Make copies of the excerpt—one for you to mark on as you model during the lesson and one for each student.

Procedures
1. If appropriate, introduce the longer text the excerpt is from, talk about the text, and read aloud just enough of the text to provide the students with adequate prior knowledge for engaging in close reading. If this is part of a thematic or content-area unit of study, activate the students' prior knowledge as needed. This phase should be short.
2. Introduce the vocabulary word and definition. Refer to the anchor chart with word and definition.
3. Introduce the purpose for close reading. Refer to the anchor chart.
4. Model close reading, thinking aloud about how you, stated as "I," are making sense of the text and what you are learning related to the purpose for close reading. (If the purpose is to identify how the civil rights activists were perseverant, only details related to this purpose should be underlined and annotated. This helps students focus clearly.) Make reference to the anchor chart with the vocabulary word defined, noting how this definition helps you explain why a particular detail is evidence. (For example, during the sixth-grade close reading lesson with the excerpt from *Marching for Freedom* [Partridge, 2009], I might say, "When I read in the text the words 'Mrs. Boynton drove to Atlanta' and asked Dr. King to help her, I realized that this was *another action she was taking* in her pursuit of voting rights. Her efforts to get voters registered had failed and, in spite of this, she was still taking steps to get voting rights for African Americans.")
5. Draw the students into a shared think-aloud, stepping in to share your own thinking as needed.
6. Release responsibility to students to closely read short chunks of text. Confer with students, coaching them to focus on the purpose for reading and identifying details related to that purpose. Regroup and ask individuals to share what they underlined and explain how it is evidence as a model for others.
7. Continue to release responsibility. (When you study the text in preparation for the lesson, you may notice points in the text where the students may struggle. Step back in to model at these points, as needed.)
8. Close by asking the students to respond to the purpose for close reading (stated as a question) orally or in writing. For example, provide all students with sticky notes and ask them to write a main idea statement, supporting evidence, and an explanation of the evidence. Another option is to engage in a "fishbowl." You and a student stand in the middle of a circle of students and model talking about what you learned related to the purpose for close reading. You make note of how you are using your notes—the annotated excerpt and the anchor chart with the definition of the word—to determine how to contribute to the conversation. Then ask students to turn to a partner and do the same.

FIGURE 8.2. Lesson plan template for introducing main or central idea vocabulary and engaging in close reading.

"How were the activists perseverant in pursuing voting rights?"

In preparation for the lesson, I spent time on the Internet reading definitions for the word *perseverant* and carefully crafted a definition I thought would be student-friendly, which I wrote on the chart as follows:

> When a person is persistent in pursuing a goal through a series of actions in spite of obstacles.

As I worked with the students, I realized that we needed to stop in the moment and clarify and deepen our understanding of the word—a couple of times. For example, after I introduced the word and shared an anecdote about a time I was perseverant, I asked small groups to share stories about when they or someone they knew had been perseverant. As I listened in on conversations about a time when they had to practice really hard to get better at basketball or do enough math problems to improve their math skills, I realized that the "obstacles" the students were identifying were all internal, related to their own mental or physical capacity for doing something, whereas the obstacles they would be identifying in the passage were external, such as other people's beliefs and actions, policies, and laws. I added details about mental obstacles and other or external obstacles to the chart, thereby expanding the students' understanding of obstacles.

I wanted the students to understand that to be perseverant is more than being persistent; it is being persistent *while taking steps toward a goal*, even when there are difficulties present. So when I created the anchor chart with the purpose for close reading, I added two questions (see Figure 7.4 on page 106):

> What actions did they take?
> What obstacles did they face?

I added these questions, despite the possible cognitive overload, because I wanted to provide additional prompts to the students who did not understand the initial prompt and also to clarify their understanding of the meaning of *perseverant*.

Later, as we engaged in close reading conversations, I realized that the students also needed a definition of *obstacles*, so I added it to the definition anchor chart: "anything that gets in the way." I clarified further by adding "help" to "series of actions" as it pertained to this excerpt and this purpose for close reading. In other words, the "series of actions" meant how the activists were *helping* African American citizens gain the right to vote. Figure 7.3 (on page 106) shows what the anchor chart looked like at the end of the lesson with the expanded definition.

What is not noted on this anchor chart is yet another conversation we had regarding the definition. Many of the students found that the "obstacles" to African Americans registering to vote were often *also* a "series of actions"; we stopped to talk about this point. In a sense, I was modeling for the students how we have to grapple with the language we use to define words; we have to think critically about definitions and how particular words such as *perseverant* can be applied as main ideas.

This approach can be used in every grade. In a fifth-grade classroom I visited at a school providing science, technology, engineering, and mathematics (STEM) curricula, every student was reading from a text set from the *Scientists in the Field Series* by Houghton Mifflin Books for Young Readers. Initially, I asked the students to write a short note to me about what scientists do. Most students used the word *study* to describe what scientists do, with very little elaboration on this point. Then I introduced the word *investigate* with the following definition on an anchor chart:

> Investigate—to examine, study, or inquire systematically in an attempt to learn the facts about something hidden, unique, or complex.

We engaged in close reading of an excerpt from *The Tarantula Scientist* (Montgomery, 2007) with the following purpose:

> How does Sam Marshall, the arachnologist, engage in the practice of investigation? What is the evidence from the text?

As we read about Sam Marshall methodically searching for goliath birdeater tarantulas in the rainforests of French Guiana in South America, we expanded the vocabulary we could use to describe a scientist's work. Figure 8.3 shows the anchor chart with the original definition and then all the words we added. Anchor charts that are co-constructed (after the initial introduction) can be very powerful in developing students' sense of agency. Amazingly, during many of the lessons described in this book, after we have co-constructed an anchor chart listing details or vocabulary we are using, many students have exhibited agency by asking me, "Can we add this word [or type of detail] to our list?"

"Try It Aloud" before Writing

Continuous assessment of the sixth-grade students' understanding (and a lot of sweat) helped me build a stronger definition for them to use as a lens for reading and thinking. We did not engage in writing beyond annotating the texts. Instead, I encouraged students to articulate orally their understanding of the word

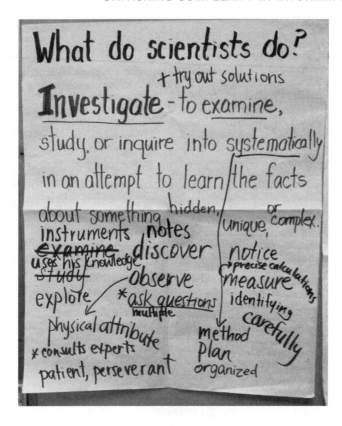

FIGURE 8.3. Anchor chart with the original definition of *investigate* and all the words we added.

perseverant and to explain the evidence they identified in the text. As described in previous chapters, there is real power in opportunities to "try out orally" what we are asking students to do in written responses. In this class, we stood in a big circle, each with our annotated response. I stood in the middle with a student volunteer, and together we modeled explaining the meaning of perseverance. Then I asked the students to turn to a partner and do the same, and I conferred with partners. Next my partner and I modeled having a conversation, identifying and *explaining* evidence from our excerpts using our expanded definition of perseverance as a lens. For this group, I even modeled looking at the definition on the anchor chart to help me come up with the language to explain my thinking. The students needed this scaffolding. As I listened to their conversations, I noticed they were using the language of our expanded definition. This language served as a hook on which to hang their thinking and helped to move their explanations forward.

Write Short Responses to Deepen Thinking about Main Ideas

In a lesson with eighth-grade students, I asked them to write explanations of evidence as part of their annotations during close reading. This class was studying the Holocaust in social studies, and we did a close reading of an excerpt from *Beyond Courage: The Untold Story of Jewish Resistance During the Holocaust* (Rappaport, 2012). (The content of this book is described further in Chapter Four.) The excerpt I chose described how some Jews in the Lithuanian ghetto at Vilna formed an organization to resist the Nazis, who were sending thousands of Jewish people to the nearby Ponar death pits. I chose this excerpt because it reveals the courage of members of this group in just a few paragraphs—as they spread the news about the organization, taught themselves how to make and also smuggled weapons into the ghetto, and so forth.

I introduced and defined the word *courage* as "the ability to do something you know is difficult or dangerous." After posting this definition as an anchor chart, I asked students to write this definition, or their own, at the tops of their papers. Similar to the previous sixth-grade lesson, I also posted the purpose for reading (written on chart paper):

How did some Jewish community members exhibit courage?

The excerpt was projected on the Smart Board. In the beginning, I underlined and wrote annotations on the text as I thought aloud or as students contributed to the group's meaning making. During these lessons, it is important to stay tightly focused on the purpose for reading. There is so much we could discuss in a text; we could spend days analyzing the many details and what they mean. However, students may easily lose their focus and their purpose for reading and become overwhelmed with how much meaning there is to absorb. In this lesson, I stayed focused on the purpose for reading. As I thought aloud, I continually returned to the prompt, asking, "Does this help me think about how some members of the Jewish community exhibited courage?"

My goal was to develop the students' sense of agency in identifying and explaining evidence—orally and in writing. As I gradually released control of the reading, and students began to read and annotate more independently, I conferred with several students. As a result of these one-to-one conversations, I was able to identify particular students who could share. (These might be students who were already on track or those who got on track as a result of our conferring—students of all abilities have the potential for sharing.) I asked individual students to come up to the Smart Board, underline the text they had underlined on their own pages, and explain to the class why they thought this underlined content revealed

Jewish community members exhibiting courage (see Figure 8.4). Then I asked students in small groups to turn to each other and explain a piece of evidence they had noted in the text. Finally, I asked all the students to put an asterisk by one piece of text they had underlined and to write an annotation that specifically explained *why* this was evidence of courage. I prompted them to use their definition of *courage*, or language from the definition, in their written responses.

Figure 8.5 shows one student's annotations on his copy of the excerpt late in the close reading experience. Even though his use of the word *dangerous* is somewhat superficial, notice how he uses the language of the definition to help him explain the evidence. The example in Figure 8.6 is a little more sophisticated. The student seems to understand the gravity of the situation when she writes *extremely*; she also addresses another dimension of courage the first student did not address: *fear*. Both students need multiple opportunities to grapple with the concept of courage. Over time, as both students have the experience of reading texts with the purpose of thinking carefully about how historical figures exhibited courage, they will become more adept at explaining their thinking.

> had a commander. All commanders took orders from Wittenberg. As in all underground groups, secrecy was critical. Not even family members were allowed to know that someone belonged to the FPO. >The word might spreed to other People then it might spread to the germans!
>
> Weapons and ammunition were bought at exorbitant prices from Lithuanian police.

FIGURE 8.4. A student's underlining and comments on the Smart Board to show textual evidence of *courage*.

> cemetery, apartment walls, wells, and water buckets. The partisan units met in the library basement. They learned how to make grenades from old lightbulbs and held target practice with unloaded guns. Strategies were created for distributing weapons and getting fighters to their posts quickly.* ShmuelKaplinski, a sanitation engineer, spent weeks underground mapping out the sewer tunnels to smuggle in weapons and, if need be, for an escape route.
>
> smuggling weapons is dangerous he could be very difficult
>
> By the fall of 1942, almost two hundred young people had joined the FPO.
>
> *= this shows courage because smuggling weapons are dangerous and the nazis could find out

FIGURE 8.5. A student's annotated excerpt from *Beyond Courage* (Rappaport, 2012).

groups, secrecy was critical. Not even family members were allowed to know that someone

belonged to the FPO. *[handwritten: It was extremely dangerous to smuggle things from Germans because if they were caught they would die. They probably feared that too]*

Weapons and ammunition were bought at exorbitant prices from Lithuanian police.

[handwritten: They could have been caught killed] Jews forced to repair German weapons smuggled arms parts into the ghetto. Unbeknownst

to the Jewish Council, FPO members were on the Jewish police force. Any time

ElchananTelerant wore a black leather coat returning from work, it signaled his comrades

in the Jewish police that he was smuggling in weapons, and they distracted the Lithuanian

guards from searching him. The arms were hidden in the ghetto library, the Jewish

FIGURE 8.6. Another student's annotated excerpt from *Beyond Courage* (Rappaport, 2012).

Provide Multiple Experiences with the Same Main Ideas during a Unit of Study

I have alluded to the idea that the lessons I have described need to be part of a series of lessons focused on a particular word or theme embedded in a rich unit of study. In a thematic or content-area-based unit of study, students have multiple opportunities to grapple with particular themes and related vocabulary. They deepen their sense of specific ideas and begin to see how those ideas can be used globally as a lens for considering other texts or events in their own lives. Once, when I was in a meeting with a group of intermediate grade teachers, a fifth-grade teacher shared with me how a theme for one of her units was "change." By the end of the unit, the students were "bonkers" with the idea of change and mentioned it throughout the day as the term applied in other contexts. She joked about how she was a little worried that they would not be able to grasp the theme for the next unit because they were so focused on the previous one. Joking aside, this is a phenomenal result. The trick is to continue expanding students' vocabulary.

The key to building vocabulary is to use a text set or group of texts that scaffolds the unit's larger ideas to facilitate understanding. It is not enough to pick any 20 books on a topic (many of them our "old favorites") to teach a unit. Instead, the titles need to be chosen intentionally. For example, in one urban school district, we planned a unit of study on the civil rights movement for third-grade students. Our essential questions were the following:

- What is social justice?
- How do beliefs influence action?

The vocabulary we introduced and used repeatedly included the following words:

segregation	*dignity*	*determined*
committed	*justice*	*protest*
courage	*nonviolence*	*perseverance*
freedom	*inspire*	*conviction*

We chose five anchor texts that supported understanding of the essential questions and use of the targeted vocabulary:

1. *My Brother Martin: A Sister Remembers Growing Up with the Rev. Dr. Martin Luther King, Jr.* (Farris, 2003).
2. *Delivering Justice: W. W. Law and the Fight for Civil Rights* (Haskins, 2008).
3. *Sit-in: How Four Friends Stood Up by Sitting Down* (Pinkney, 2010).
4. *March On! The Day My Brother Martin Changed the World* (Farris, 2008).
5. *Harvesting Hope: The Story of Cesar Chavez* (Krull, 2003).

Ideally, each anchor text would be used for a series of three to five lessons for multiple purposes, including the following:

- Reading aloud and asking higher-level questions to build meaning around main ideas.
- Using an excerpt for close reading for the purpose of identifying evidence to support main ideas.
- Using an excerpt of an important event in the book (that revealed a main idea) to create a Reader's Theater script.
- Using content from the anchor text to devise a prompt for writing a response (related to the main ideas).

In addition, we developed a leveled text set of books about civil rights organizers, with texts written at a variety of levels so diverse learners could access the content during guided reading groups or while reading with a partner or independently.

Our goal was to create a 90- to 120-minute literacy block that immersed students in studying this period. Every text we chose and every lesson we created was focused on the essential questions—and on expanding the students' vocabulary, aiding their ability to answer those essential questions.

Closing Thoughts

Reading and learning from informational texts empower our students. In order for students to become skilled readers and learners, however, we educators have to be present—stepping in and stepping back as the students grapple with these texts. The key to this process is our own knowledge of how these texts work and what might make them complex for particular students.

To summarize the points made in this book, I have provided the following two tables. Table 1 (pp. 126–129) includes a list of the "dimensions" or "parts" of a complex text that have been examined in these chapters. Table 2 (pp. 129–132) offers a brief description of the instructional methods I have recommended. For me, this inquiry into text complexity and effective teaching of informational texts is not over. I encourage you to continue the conversation with me through my website and blog at *www.sunday-cummins.com*.

TABLE 1. Dimensions of a Text's Complexity

<u>Purpose and Ideas</u>

Author's purpose

The author's purpose is the reason why the author wrote the text. Frequently, authors have more than one purpose for writing a text. These purposes, or genres, are not always explicitly stated in a text. These purposes fall into five categories:

1. To instruct.
2. To recount.
3. To explain.
4. To describe.
5. To persuade.

Main or central ideas

The main idea at the *gist* level of a text is a short summary that conveys a bigger idea or important point in a text or even a section of text. The main idea at the *theme* level of a text is a global idea that can be applied to the text in hand as well as to other texts. Constructing a main idea is about noticing the relationships between ideas in a text.

Idea density and difficulty

An author may include a lot of ideas or details in a compact or short section of text. If the text is well crafted and tailored to be accessible, the ideas, while still rigorous, should still be accessible to a well-matched audience. However, if the author assumes too much of his or her audience developmentally and covers too much content, with very little development of ideas, the text may be too hard for age-appropriate readers.

<u>Structure</u>

Traditional structures at macro and micro levels

A text's structure is how a text is built—and how its components are arranged and are interrelated. A text's structure is determined by the author's purpose. Commonly taught structures include:

- Enumerative.
- Sequence/chronology/narrative.
- Comparison.
- Causal relationships.
- Problem–solution.

Complex texts for intermediate and middle grade readers, for the most part, are not pure structures. Readers need to think flexibly about these structures. Authors use these structures in many ways based on their purpose. Enumerative, sequence/chronology/ narrative, and problem–solution are frequently macro structures (i.e., the structure for a whole text). Short sections of a larger text might be structured as a sequence, comparison, or causal relationship.

(continued)

TABLE 1. *(continued)*

Types of details in non-narrative texts

Authors employ types of details at the micro or sentence level. The author's purpose continues to drive the development of the text even at this level. Details that occur frequently in non-narrative texts on science topics include details about the following:

- Systems (e.g., the digestive system).
- Mechanisms (e.g., the toilet and how it works).
- Processes (e.g., how a seed becomes a plant).

Discussions that involve noticing and naming types of details authors use can be led about any topic (e.g., animals, land forms, cultures, steps for voting or getting a law passed) and about a text written for any purpose (e.g., a persuasive essay). Details unique to a text may surface as well; there is no right or wrong way to name these details. The point is to think about what the author is doing with language to convey an idea.

Types of details in narrative texts

Although there is some overlap with non-narrative texts, authors of narratives about historical figures or events and about the work of scientists and engineers also utilize details about agents of change such as (but not limited to) the following:

- Name of the agent.
- The agent's context.
- The agent's character.
- The agent's disposition.
- Actions the agent takes.

Authors also employ the craft of writing traditionally attributed to fiction. For example, an author may use figurative language and flashbacks to develop an idea. In addition, particular details reveal an author's bias.

Conversations about how these details (as well as the details in non-narrative texts) are woven together and how they support each other are vital to strengthening a reader's ability to identify main or central ideas.

Multimodality

There are multiple modes, used for a variety of purposes, in informational texts. There is the visual mode that includes the running text, the features, and how these two aspects are designed and laid out. Online texts contain additional modes in which a text or information can be experienced with video and audio clips. Many of these texts can be interacted with and marked up by the reader as well, providing another way to experience the text.

Features

Features are distinguishable parts of a text that serve to weave together the multitude of other parts in a text, helping readers access the main ideas. Features such as photographs and illustrations provide visual access and support or extend the ideas in the text. Features such as headings and subheadings help the reader locate information in a text.

(continued)

TABLE 1. *(continued)*

Layout and design

The layout of a text is the way in which the parts of a text—such as the features, the extended text, and the key words in bold print—are positioned on the page. The design is the purpose and planning behind the layout. Layouts are intended to be attractive and catch the reader's eye. More important, though, a page's layout is carefully planned to serve the author's purpose and provide a way for aspects of the text and the ideas they convey to be presented cohesively.

Language and Vocabulary

Register and tone

Register, or style, is a particular type of language used for a particular purpose. The tone of the text is the way the author expresses his or her attitude through the text. In what we might consider traditional informational texts, the register is frequently formal and the tone is distant, unemotional, and objective. Currently, there is a trend in informational texts in which authors use less formal registers, drawing their readers into conversations with humorous or intimate tones.

General academic vocabulary, including connectives

Academic vocabulary is generally vocabulary associated with schooling and that is not content-area specific. Examples include terms such as *evaluate, investigate,* and *text structure.* These terms occur relatively frequently in many classroom contexts. Authors use particular words and phrases, called *connectives,* to link ideas in a text. These words serve to reveal the relationship between ideas, contributing to the cohesion of a text. Categories of connectives include:

- Additive
- Temporal
- Causal
- Adversative

Domain-specific vocabulary

Informational-text authors rely heavily on domain-specific vocabulary to expand on and develop ideas. These are content-area words (e.g., *worker bee, nurse bee,* and *larva royal jelly*) that students may not see very often when they are reading broadly, but will see several times during a unit of study on a particular topic or issue.

Knowledge Demands

Background knowledge

Students' background knowledge is generally considered the knowledge they have developed as part of life experiences outside of the school classroom. As we know, these experiences vary widely and tapping them might or might not be of use in understanding informational texts. Many authors of informational texts do try to help their readers use background knowledge to grapple with conceptually difficult ideas. The difficulty is that background knowledge is not universal, and attempts to connect with readers, such as

(continued)

TABLE 1. *(continued)*

referring to snowballs as a way to explain the force of gravity, may only be helpful to audiences with particular experiences.

Prior knowledge

Prior knowledge is information or skills acquired during school experiences; it is formal academic or domain-specific knowledge. Sometimes authors may assume students' prior knowledge. However, if some students do not have this prior knowledge, the text becomes more complex.

Disciplinary viewpoint

Many authors are experts in their field and write with a disciplinary point of view. The disciplinary viewpoint assumes an understanding by the reader of ways of thinking and creating knowledge that are inherent to the author's field. For example, scientists and engineers engage in inquiry through investigating, evaluating, and developing explanations and solutions. An author in this field may not state this process explicitly, assuming that the reader understands it and will use this understanding to interpret the ideas in the text.

TABLE 2. Instructional Methods for Unpacking a Text's Complexity

Approach	Explanation
Integrate and use consistently the language of informational texts.	Distinguish the difference between terms such as *author's purpose*, *author's main* or *central idea*, and *text structure*. Define these terms on anchor charts as visual support. Carefully and intentionally use these terms as part of your text introductions and conversations. Examples of definitions and specific language to use are located in Tables 2.1, 3.1, and 4.1 and Figures 6.1 and 8.1.
Co-create anchor charts with students that expand over a series of lessons.	Create an initial anchor chart (for a designated purpose, such as defining a vocabulary term, stating the author's purpose, or stating the purpose for close reading). Keep charts posted as visuals for you and the students to refer to during close reading of excerpts, conversations about text, and opportunities for writing. Add to these charts as students' thinking expands. See examples of anchor charts in Figures 3.1, 3.2, 5.4, 5.10, 6.3, 7.3, 7.4, and 8.3.
Read aloud informational texts regularly.	In second through eighth grade, read aloud to students from informational texts. State the author's purpose and, if appropriate, the students' purpose for listening. Ideally, these texts are aligned with an integrated or content area of study, extending students' knowledge as well as providing experiences for students to develop an understanding of what informational texts "sound like." These texts can also be used as anchor texts for choosing close reading excerpts and additional texts for students to read with a partner or independently. Recommendations for high-quality texts to read aloud can be found at my blog at *www.Sunday-Cummins.com*.

(continued)

TABLE 2. *(continued)*

Approach	Explanation
Teach the dimensions of text complexity as part of integrated or content-area units of study that nurture a transfer of learning.	Students need to understand that examining a text's complexity is not an isolated learning experience in the classroom. Instead, there is generative value in this experience in that their growing knowledge of what makes a text complex can be used to help them think through and learn from other texts on the same topic. This knowledge serves to develop students' sense of agency and identity as strategic readers of complex text. Many of the lessons described in this book were part of integrated units of study. For an explanation of a cycle of lessons that incorporated teacher-chosen excerpts as well as texts at students' instructional level (from a text set), see the section "'Transfer' Learning to Other Topics or Theme-Related Texts" in Chapter Five (p. 76).
Immerse students in reading from text sets as part of a unit of study.	Provide regular opportunities for students to develop stamina for reading complex text. These opportunities should include reading longer texts as well as reading multiple texts on the same topic or issues. For an example of a text set, see the section "Provide Multiple Experiences with the Same Main Ideas during a Unit of Study" in Chapter Eight (p. 123).
Provide experiences when students can "notice and name" dimensions of text complexity.	Use a constructivist approach, providing opportunities for students to notice a particular dimension of a text's complexity, such as a text's structure or the types of details an author uses. Step in at the point of need to name these dimensions. This might be done during a close reading lesson or during an individual conference with students.
Use close reading as a way to think more deeply about a dimension of text complexity.	Choose an excerpt of text for close reading. (The length of the excerpt will depend on the developmental needs of students and your purpose for close reading.) During the lesson, incorporate the following: • Project the text for all students to view. • Provide a copy for all students. • Clearly state (and post) the purpose for close reading. • Think aloud about how you are making meaning of the text (initially); annotate the text as visual access to what you have said orally during the think-aloud. • Draw the students into a shared think-aloud and shared writing of annotations. • If appropriate, begin or add to an anchor chart to document the kinds of annotations you and the students are making.

(continued)

TABLE 2. *(continued)*

Approach	Explanation
	• Gradually release responsibility, conferring with individual students and small groups, stepping in at the point of need. • Continually refer to the purpose for close reading during conversations and shared writing of annotations. • Regroup. Engage students in orally discussing what they learned related to their purpose for close reading as well as short, related writing experiences. As much as possible, close reading should occur in small groups. For examples, see descriptions of lessons in Chapter Five (pp. 73–86), Chapter Six (pp. 92–95), Chapter Seven (pp. 104–106), and Chapter Eight (pp. 115–118, 121–123).
Study texts before teaching.	Although we want to challenge students to grapple with complex texts and develop stamina for doing this, we still need to understand what makes these texts complex. In preparation for close reading, read the text excerpt multiple times, making sense of its complexity. With the purpose for close reading in mind, annotate the text. Use these notes as a reference during close reading instruction. For an example of notes I have prepared, see Figure 5.3 on page 74.
Use small-group conversations as a tool for deepening students' understanding of content and a text's complexity.	Ask students to use their annotated notes or written responses to texts read independently or with a partner to guide their conversations about a selected text's content and/or a dimension of complexity (e.g., development of a main or central idea). Coach students as needed, including modeling a conversation by asking a student to come to the front with his or her notes. Model having a conversation, referring to the purpose for close reading or the prompt for critical thinking conversations. Model referring to the annotations on the projected text excerpt and the annotations the student made on his or her copy of the excerpt. For an explanation of how I incorporate these experiences into lessons, see the section "'Try It Aloud' before Writing" in Chapter Eight (p. 119).
Use writing as a tool for students to synthesize their understanding of a text's complexity or the content they learned related to the purpose for close reading.	Provide opportunities for students to sketch and write short responses related to the purpose for close reading. Some of these experiences can be short and simple, such as writing a claim with an explanation of supporting evidence. As needed, model how to write in response to the purpose for close reading. For examples of students' responses, see figures showing student work in Chapters Three, Four, Five, and Eight.

(continued)

TABLE 2. *(continued)*

Approach	Explanation
Observe students closely during instruction and make instructional shifts as needed.	Confer closely with students, helping them name what they are noticing and asking questions that elicit extended responses related to the purpose for close reading. Use this information to assess understanding. As needed, take advantage of teachable moments, stepping back in to instruct at the point of need. For examples of lessons describing how I exploited teachable moments, see the following: • Chapter Four (pp. 61–62), regarding a lesson with fifth graders on text structure. • Chapter Five (pp. 73–76), with second graders who needed guidance in how to sketch using their annotations. • Chapter Five (pp. 82–86), during a lesson with seventh-grade students on the credibility of authors' details. • Chapter Eight (pp. 115–119), where I explain how I expanded students' understanding of the word *perseverant* as I assessed their conversations and responses.

APPENDIX

Study Guide

This study guide has been developed to promote a deeper understanding of the dimensions of text complexity and an increased capacity for supporting students who are grappling with these texts. Although individual educators may find this guide helpful, the suggestions are geared toward professional learning communities (PLCs). Exercises and prompts for conversations are included for each chapter; readers can follow them in a sequence or skip to particular chapters. The objective of this guide is to nurture conversations helpful to readers' everyday practice. As part of that endeavor, in each section of the guide I suggest bringing to meetings sample informational texts and other instructional materials, teaching artifacts, and student work samples.

Chapter One. What Do We Mean by Text Complexity?

1. Independently or with your colleagues, define the term *text complexity*. (Consider doing this before reading Chapter One.) What is easy as well as difficult about applying this concept in choosing texts for classroom instruction?

2. Before or after reading Chapter One, engage in a conversation regarding the following question, "What would make articulating the meaning of the term *text complexity* easier?" Consider using this conversation as a launching point for studying the rest of this book, returning to this question at multiple points to reflect on how the content of this book and shifts in classroom practice clarify the meaning of *text complexity*.

Chapter Two. What Makes an Informational Text Complex?

1. After reading this chapter, choose an informational text that might be used to teach in the near future. Read the text or an excerpt from it (with a group of peers, if possible) and then reread and analyze the text while examining the dimensions of text complexity explained in this chapter. Use the analyses of texts described in Chapter Two as a model for articulating the dimensions of the text being examined.

2. Over the course of several meetings or study sessions, examine multiple texts. These meetings might be short 10- to 20-minute conversations, and you can choose a focus

dimension for the discussion, such as "How does the layout and design of this article contribute to the central ideas in the text?" For some texts and focus dimensions, short excerpts of a longer text might be appropriate. The objective here is to develop a capacity for describing the complexity of an informational text. Consider closing each conversation with a reflection on how PLC members' understanding of a text's complexity deepened as a result of the discussion.

Examples of questions (aligned with particular dimensions) for short discussions include the following:

Questions about Purpose and Ideas
- What is the author's purpose?
- What is the main idea? At the gist level? At the theme level?
- What is the density of the ideas in a short excerpt of the text? If there appears to be a dense amount of information in the excerpt, is it manageable given the quality of the author's writing?

Questions about a Text's Structure
- Regarding the running text—
  o Is there an apparent traditional text structure?
  o Does the author use a variety of details to build the ideas or a deeper understanding of the topic?
- Regarding the mode of the text—
  o How do the different modes (visual and auditory) contribute to the development of ideas in the text?
- Regarding the layout and design of the text—
  o What is the layout of the text?
  o How is the text designed to create a cohesive idea?

Questions about Language and Vocabulary
- What is the register and tone of the text? How do these elements contribute to the appeal of the text? How do they reinforce the author's ideas?
- What is the important academic vocabulary in this text? Are there connectives in the text? What role do these connectives play in building ideas?
- What is the important domain-specific vocabulary in this text? What does the author assume about a reader's understanding of particular vocabulary words?

Questions about Knowledge Demands
- How does the author try to connect with the reader's background knowledge or prior experiences?
  o Does the author use register and tone to engage the reader?
  o Does the author employ comparisons with common objects or experiences?
  o What does the author assume about his or her audience's life experiences?
- Does the author assume some content knowledge? What details in the text reveal this assumption?

- How does the author reveal a disciplinary viewpoint? What does he or she reveal about how knowledge is created in his or her field?

3. For critical insight into the Common Core authors' (potentially dangerous) assumptions about text complexity, read and discuss the chapter "Examining Three Assumptions about Text Complexity: Standard 10 of the Common Core" (Hiebert & Van Sluys, 2014). This chapter is accessible at *http://textproject.org/library/articles/examining-three-assumptions-about-text-complexity*. The authors contend that these assumptions in the Common Core State Standards may lead to an increase in the achievement gap if not addressed by educators and policymakers.

Chapter Three. What Do We Mean by an Author's Purpose?

1. After reading this chapter, choose several texts that might be used in the near future to teach. Practice articulating, orally and in writing, the purpose of these texts. Use the language of purpose:

- To instruct.
- To recount.
- To explain.
- To or describe.
- To persuade.

In a conversation with peers, consider the following question: *How might this language provide a scaffold for students?*

2. Review the "Recommendations for Instruction" at the end of Chapter Three. Continue to intentionally use the language of the author's purpose with students through the following activities:

- Create anchor charts with the "author's purpose" for important texts that small groups of students or the entire class will be reading for themselves or listening to being read aloud. If needed, use Figures 3.1 and 3.2 as models for charts.
- With a small group of students, try having a conversation about the author's purpose. After the students have read and discussed an informational text, ask them "What do you think the author's purpose was for writing this text?" As the students share, find opportunities to contribute to their thinking by naming the author's purpose that emerges in the discussion. For example, if a student is sharing how the author stated facts about the dolphin's diet, where it lives, and so forth, say, "So the author's purpose is to *describe* the dolphin." As different purposes emerge and are named, write each purpose with details from the text on a sheet of paper for the students to view. See Figure 3.4 as an example.

Return to the PLC with instructional artifacts and discuss the value of these learning experiences for students.

3. Engage in conversation or reflection about this question: *When we ask students to state the author's purpose, how do we avoid having this task become a mindless fill-in-the-blank exercise for them?*

Chapter Four. What Do We Mean by a Text's Structure?

1. Choose a text to examine (individually or with a group). Start by identifying the author's purpose. Then continue by analyzing the text's structure. The following questions might be helpful:
   - Does the author employ one or more of the traditional structures at the macro level? And if so, how?
     o Enumerative.
     o Sequence/chronology/narrative.
     o Comparison.
     o Causal relationships.
     o Problem–solution.
   - How does the structure of the text support the author's purpose for writing the text?

2. Choose an excerpt from the text to analyze at the micro level (i.e., the section, paragraph, or sentence level). Does the author employ sequence, comparison, and causal relationships at the micro level? If so, how? What is the author's purpose for using a particular structure at the micro level?

3. Review the lesson-plan template in Figure 4.2 as well as the "Recommendations for Instruction" at the end of Chapter Four. During instruction, what might be done to help students notice and name a text's structure? Consider the needs of the students as well as the complexity of the text and how a reader-to-text match can be made through intentional planning. Plan a lesson and return to the PLC with instructional artifacts. What happened for the students during this learning experience? How did the students reveal learning?

Chapter Five. What Types of Details Are in Non-Narrative Texts?

1. With a group of colleagues or independently, choose an excerpt of text that is non-narrative. Identify the author's purpose and main idea or topic. Then engage in a close reading to notice and name the types of details the author uses to build an understanding of the topic or main idea. Use Figure 5.7 as a reference. Some details may seem unfamiliar or are not addressed in this book; grapple with those details, contemplating the author's purpose for using a particular type of detail, and naming as appropriate.

2. Review the lesson plan templates in Figures 5.7 and 5.13. Plan a lesson or series of lessons to model and gradually release close reading for types of details in a particular text excerpt. The lesson can include the following components:
   - Reading aloud from an anchor text (related to the unit of study).
   - Engaging students in shared or independent reading of an excerpt from the anchor text, with the text projected for all students to view and a copy of the excerpt for each student.
   - Thinking aloud, as you model noticing and naming the types of details in the text and charting those details. Gradually engage students in a shared think-aloud and charting of details.

- Coaching students as they attempt to notice and name details with a partner or independently.
- If appropriate, modeling for students how to use the text to decide what to sketch and then releasing responsibility of sketching to the students or modeling how to write a summary and synthesis using the language of the types of details the author employed.

3. Return to the next PLC meeting with instructional artifacts to share, such as the chart with the list of details and the copy of the excerpt used to model identifying types of details and examples of student work. Examine the student work samples and discuss the following:

- What types of details do the students appear to notice independently?
- What types of details does the teacher need to continue noticing and naming?
- How does the sketch or written synthesis reveal understanding of the content?
- What does follow-up instruction need to look like?

Chapter Six. What Types of Details Are in Narrative Texts?

1. With a group or independently, choose an excerpt of text that is written primarily as a narrative. Identify the author's purpose and main idea. Then engage in a close reading to notice and name the author's craft—specifically, what he or she does to develop an idea. Use Figure 6.1 as a reference.

2. Plan a lesson to model and gradually release close reading for the author's craft, specifically the types of details he or she employs, in a particular text excerpt.

3. Assess the students' annotations. Are they recognizing the types of details modeled on their own? Do the annotations reveal an understanding of craft versus the content of the text excerpt? How do the annotations reveal a deeper understanding of the main or central idea in the text?

Chapter Seven. Why Pay Attention to Connective Language?

Choose an excerpt of text to read closely with students for a particular purpose: for example, for identifying the main idea and supporting evidence or for identifying the types of details an author has used.

1. In this excerpt, identify the connectives the author has used. Use Figure 7.1 as a reference. Independently or with the PLC, define these connectives in kid-friendly terms. What language will be used to clarify the meaning of the connective and how does it reveal the relationship between ideas in a text?

2. Implement the close reading lesson, stopping to highlight the value of noticing and identifying the purpose of the connectives. Ask the students to share aloud or write a short response to how thinking about a particular connective helped them understand the text better.

3. If appropriate, begin an anchor chart with a list of connectives and student-friendly definitions as these words are encountered during close reading.

4. Over a series of lessons, continue to notice the connectives and explain the purpose of particular ones. Observe for students' increased awareness of these words.

5. Return to the PLC with notes about the lessons.

   • What were the benefits of these conversations during close reading with students?
   • What remain as obstacles?
   • What should follow-up instruction look like?

6. For information related to students' understanding of connectives, read the journal article "Connectives: Fitting Another Piece of the Vocabulary Instruction Puzzle" (Crosson & Lesaux, 2013). Based on their research, the authors provide insight into the benefits of teaching the language of connectives to English learners as well as native English speakers.

Chapter Eight. How Are Main Ideas Constructed?

1. Over the course of several meetings, closely read short texts and identify the main or central ideas at the gist or text level and at the theme or global level. Table 8.1 can be used as a reference. Practice writing the main-idea statements with key vocabulary terms that might be defined and explored during a lesson.

2. Review the lessons described in Chapter Eight, "Recommendations for Instruction," and the lesson template explained in Figure 8.2.

3. Consider starting a "main idea" or "central idea" word wall that can be added to and revised over the course of several lessons in a unit of study with students.

4. Plan a lesson for close reading with a main idea that is already identified. The main idea should include a key vocabulary word such as *perseverant, destructive,* or *courageous.* (See Figures 7.3 and 8.3 as a reference.) The purpose for close reading should be to identify and explain evidence that supports the main idea. Create an anchor chart with a language-rich, student-friendly definition.

5. In preparation, study the excerpt, underlining key words and phrases that support making sense of the main idea and the key vocabulary word. Annotate in the margins of the text how the underlined text explains the main idea; integrate the language of the defined vocabulary word into the explanations.

6. Implement the lesson. Stay focused on the purpose for close reading and the defined vocabulary word. The lesson should include components similar to those listed in Figure 8.2.

7. Collect the students' annotated excerpts and, if appropriate, bring a student sample to the next PLC meeting. Discuss the students' annotations:

   • How did each student appropriate the language of the definition?
   • What do the annotations reveal about students' understanding of the content of the text?

8. For additional examples and resources related to close-reading lessons focused on the main or central idea of a text excerpt, visit *www.Sunday-Cummins.com.*

References

Adler, D. A. (2013). *Things that float and things that don't*. New York: Holiday House.

Alarcón, F. X. (2008). *Animal poems of the Iguazu/Animalario del Iguazu* (English and Spanish Edition). New York: Children's Book Press.

Anastasia, L. (2013). The real cost of fashion. *Junior Scholastic Current Events, 116*(1). Retrieved February 5, 2014, from *http://junior.scholastic.com/issues/09_02_13/book#/6*.

Anderson, T. H., & Armbruster, B. B. (1984). Content area textbooks. In R. C. Anderson, J. Osborn, & R. J. Tierney (Eds.), *Learning to read in American schools: Basal readers and content texts* (pp. 193–226). Hillsdale, NJ: Erlbaum.

Aronson, M. (2011). *Trapped: How the world rescued 33 miners from 2,000 feet below the Chilean desert*. New York: Atheneum Books for Young Readers.

Banting, E. (2012). *England: The land*. New York: Crabtree.

Bausum, A. (2012). *Marching to the mountaintop: How poverty, labor fights, and the civil rights set the stage for Martin Luther King, Jr.'s final hours*. Washington, DC: National Geographic.

Beck, I. L., McKeown, M. G., & Kucan, L. (2013). *Bringing words to life: Robust vocabulary instruction* (2nd ed.). New York: Guilford Press.

Bishop, N. (2007). *Spiders*. New York: Scholastic.

Bishop, N. (2008). *Frogs*. New York: Scholastic.

Bishop, N. (2012). *Snakes*. New York: Scholastic.

Bix, C. O. (2013, March). Beetle quest. *National Geographic Explorer! Pioneer Edition, 12*(5), pp. 2–9.

Blumenthal, K. (2011). *Bootleg: Murder, moonshine, and the lawless years of Prohibition*. New York: Roaring Book Press.

Bragg, G. (2012). *How they croaked: The awful ends of the awfully famous*. New York: Walker.

Cate, A. L. (2013). *Look up! Bird-watching in your own backyard*. Somerville, MA: Candlewick Press.

Cohen, M. (2010). *Genetic engineering*. New York: Crabtree.

Crosson, A. C., & Lesaux, N. K. (2013). Connectives: Fitting another piece of the vocabulary instruction puzzle. *The Reading Teacher, 67*(3), 193–200.

Cummins, S. (2013). *Close reading of informational texts: Assessment-driven instruction in grades 3–8*. New York: Guilford Press.

Cunningham, J. W., & Moore, D. W. (1986). The confused world of main ideas. In J. F. Baumann (Ed.), *Teaching main idea comprehension* (pp. 1–17). Newark, DE: International Reading Association.

Deardoff, J. (2011, March 18). Cell phone radiation could pose dangers to kids. *Chicago Tribune*. Retrieved from *http://articles.chicagotribune.com/2011-03-18/features/chi-cell-phones-could-pose-dangers-to-kids-20110318_1_cell-phone-radiation-brain-activity*.

DeCristofano, C. C. (2012). *A black hole is NOT a hole*. Watertown, MA: Charlesbridge.

Fang, Z., & Pace, B. G. (2013). Teaching with challenging texts in the disciplines: Text complexity and close reading. *Journal of Adolescent and Adult Literacy, 57*(2), 104–108.

Farris, C. K. (2003). *My brother Martin: A sister remembers growing up with the Rev. Dr. Martin Luther King Jr.* New York: Simon & Schuster Books for Young Readers.

Farris, C. K. (2008). *March on!: The day my brother Martin changed the world*. New York: Scholastic.

Floca, B. (2013). *Locomotive*. New York: Atheneum Books for Young Readers.

Freedman, R. (2014). *Angel Island: Gateway to gold mountain*. New York: Clarion

Geiger, B. (2010). Active earth. *National Geographic Explorer! Pathfinder Edition, 10*(1), 8–13.

Geiger, B. (2013). Extreme ice. *National Geographic Explorer! Pioneer Edition, 12*(4), 15–23.

George, J. C. (2008). *The wolves are back*. New York: Dutton Children's Books.

Gibbons, G. (1991). *From seed to plant*. New York: Holiday House.

Gilbert, G. (2010). The winning edge. *National Geographic Explorer! Pathfinder Edition, 10*(1), 14–17.

Goldish, M. (2008). *Gray wolves: Return to Yellowstone (America's animal comebacks series)*. New York: Bearport.

Gray, L. (2013). *Giant Pacific octopus: The world's largest octopus*. New York: Bearport.

Hague, B. (2012). *Alien deep: Revealing the mysterious living world at the bottom of the ocean*. Washington, DC: National Geographic Society.

Haskins, J. (2008). *Delivering justice: W. W. Law and the fight for civil rights*. Cambridge, MA: Candlewick Press.

Heiligman, D. (2002). *Honeybees*. Washington, DC: National Geographic Society.

Heos, B. (2013). *Stronger than steel: Spider silk DNA and the quest for better bulletproof vests, sutures, and parachute rope*. New York: Houghton Mifflin.

Hewitt, S. (2009). *Waste and recycling*. New York: Crabtree.

Hiebert, E. H., & Mesmer, H. A. E. (2013). Upping the ante of text complexity in the Common Core State Standards: Examining its potential impact on young readers. *Educational Researcher, 42*(1), 44–51.

Hiebert, E. H., & Van Sluys, K. (2014). Examining three assumptions about text complexity: Standard 10 of the Common Core State Standards. In K. S. Goodman, R. C. Calfee, & Y. M. Goodman (Eds.), *Whose knowledge counts in government literacy policies?: Why expertise matters* (pp. 144–160). New York: Routledge.

Hopkinson, D. (2012). *Titanic: Voices from the disaster*. New York: Scholastic Press.

Houghton Mifflin Harcourt. (2013). *Stronger than steel: Spider silk DNA and the quest for better bulletproof vests, sutures, and parachute rope*. Retrieved February 11, 2014, from *www.hmhco.com/shop/books/Stronger-Than-Steel/9780547681269*.

Jacobson, S., & Colón, E. (2006). *The 9/11 report: A graphic adaptation*. New York: Hill and Wang.

Johnston, P. H. (2004). *Choice words: How our language affects children's learning*. Portland, ME: Stenhouse.

Kirby, P. F. (2009). *What bluebirds do*. Honesdale, PA: Boyds Mill Press.

Krull, K. (2003). *Harvesting hope: The story of Cesar Chavez*. New York: Harcourt.

Macaulay, D. (2013). *Toilet: How it works*. New York: David Macaulay Studio McMillan Children's Publishing Group.

Markle, S. (2012). *The case of the vanishing golden frogs: A scientific mystery*. Minneapolis, MN: Millbrook Press.

McClafferty, C. K. (2011). *The many faces of George Washington: Remaking a presidential icon*. Minneapolis, MN: Carolrhoda Books.

Merriam-Webster.com. (n.d.). Definitions retrieved February 4–18, 2014, from *www.merriam-webster.com*.

Metametrics, Inc. (2014a). *The Lexile framework for reading: Nic Bishop Spiders*. Retrieved February 11, 2014, from *www.lexile.com/book/details/9780439877565*.

Metametrics, Inc. (2014b). *The Lexile framework for reading: Stronger than steel*. Retrieved February 11, 2014, from *www.lexile.com/book/details/9780547681269*.

Miller, G. (2012). Super survivors. *National Geographic Explorer! Pathfinder Edition, 11*(5), 16–21.

Mis, M. S. (2009). *Exploring glaciers*. New York: Power Kids Press.

Montgomery, S. (2007). *The tarantula scientists (Scientists in the field series)*. New York: Houghton Mifflin Company.

Moore, K. (1997). *If you lived at the time of the American Revolution (If you series)*. New York: Scholastic.

Murphy, J. (2010). *The great fire*. New York: Scholastic.

Murray, P. (1996). *Volcanoes*. North Mankato, MN: Child's World

National Governors Association Center for Best Practices and Council of Chief State School Officers. (2010). *Common Core State Standards for English language arts and literacy in history/social studies, science, and technical subjects*. Washington, DC: Author.

Nelson, K. (2011). *Heart and soul: The story of America and African Americans*. New York: HarperCollins.

Nobleman, M. T. (2008). *The Triangle Shirtwaist Factory fire (we the people series)*. Minneapolis, MN: Compass Point Books.

O'Connell, C., & Jackson, D. M. (2011). *The elephant scientist (Scientists in the field series)*. New York: Houghton Mifflin Books for Children.

Ornes, S. (2011, April 7). Cell phones on the brain. *Science News for Students*. Retrieved from *https://student.societyforscience.org/article/cell-phones-brain*.

Partridge, E. (2009). *Marching for freedom: Walk together, children, and don't you grow weary*. New York: Penguin.

Pearson, P. D., & Johnson, D. D. (1978). *Teaching reading comprehension*. New York: Holt, Rinehart & Winston.

Pinkney, A. D. (2010). *Sit-in: How four friends stood up by sitting down*. New York: Little, Brown and Company.

Raloff, J. (2013, February 17). Aquatic predators affect carbon-storing plant life. *Science News for Students*. Retrieved from *www.sciencenews.org/article/aquatic-predators-affect-carbon-storing-plant-life*.

Rappaport, D. (2012). *Beyond courage: The untold story of Jewish resistance during the Holocaust*. Somerville, MA: Candlewick Press.

Robinson, F. (2013). *The aye-aye*. Portsmouth, NH: Heinemann.

Samaras, T. (2012). In the strike zone. *National Geographic Explorer! Pathfinder Edition, 11*(5), 10–15.

Sandler, M. W. (2009). *The dust bowl through the lens: How photography revealed and helped remedy a national disaster*. New York: Walker.

Sands, S. (2002). *Kids Discover: Aztecs*. New York: Kids Discover.

Scholastic. (2014). *Scholastic Store: Nic Bishop Spiders*. Retrieved February 11, 2014, from *http://store.scholastic.com/Books/Hardcovers/Nic-Bishop-Spiders*.

Senior, K. (2002). *You wouldn't want to be sick in the 16th century: Diseases you'd rather not catch*. New York: Scholastic.

Shores, E. L. (2011). *How to make bubbles*. Mankato, MN: Capstone Press.

Simon, S. (2000). *Bones: Our skeletal system*. New York: HarperCollins.

Simon, S. (2005). *Guts: Our digestive system*. New York: HarperCollins.

Simon, S. (2006a). *The brain: Our nervous system*. New York: HarperCollins.

Simon, S. (2006b). *The heart: Our circulatory system*. New York: HarperCollins.

Stewart, M. (2014). *How does the ear hear?: And other questions about the five senses*. New York: Sterling Children's Books.

Symes, R. F. (1988). *Rocks and minerals (Eyewitness series)*. New York: Alfred A. Knopf.

Turner, P. S. (2013). *The dolphins of Shark Bay (Scientists in the field series)*. New York: Houghton Mifflin Harcourt Books for Young Readers.

Walker, S. M. (2011). *Blizzard of glass: The Halifax explosion of 1917*. New York: Henry Holt.

Wedner, D. (2012). Got poison? *National Geographic Explorer! Pathfinder Edition, 11*(5), 2–9.

West, T. (2009). *Planet Earth scrapbook: Amazing animals of the rainforest*. New York: Scholastic.

Wick, W. (1997). *A drop of water: A book of science and wonder*. New York: Scholastic Press.

Wiggins, G., & McTighe, J. (2005). *Understanding by design* (expanded 2nd ed.). Upper Saddle River, NJ: Pearson.

Index

Page numbers in italics indicate tables or figures.